I0539531

NOW
- Navigate Our World -
Notitia Omnium Wissenschaftia

Written by
Waid Sainvil

Preface

"Now" is a versatile word in language, serving as an adverb, conjunction, and informal adjective, each with distinct meanings and applications. As an adverb, "now" indicates the present time or moment, often used synonymously with phrases like "at the moment," "at present," or "right now." This usage emphasizes immediacy and contemporaneity, as exemplified in phrases such as "where are you living now?" which pinpoint a specific temporal context with urgency and relevance.

In conversational contexts, "now" also functions as a conjunction to emphasize a particular statement or moment within a narrative. For example, one might assert, "now, my first impulse was to run away," highlighting a crucial decision or thought in their personal narrative. This application directs attention to a precise instance, intensifying emphasis and coherence in storytelling.

Informally, "now" operates as an adjective to describe what is fashionable or currently trending. It reflects contemporary trends or styles deemed modern or up-to-date within a specific cultural or social context. For instance, referring to seventies disco dancing as "very now" suggests its current appeal or relevance, aligning with prevailing tastes and societal norms.

In a literary or thematic sense, the intentional use of the acronym "NOW" in my book underscores its significance and memorability. This acronymic approach directs readers or listeners toward the core themes or messages of the work, ensuring clarity and resonance in communicating its essence.

The Latin acronym NOW, "Notitia Omnium Wissenschaftia," translates to "Knowledge of All Sciences." It combines the meanings of its components: "Notitia" for knowledge or acquaintance, "Omnium" for all, and "Wissenschaftia," a Latinized term derived from German, representing science or knowledge. Thus, "Notitia Omnium Wissenschaftia" conveys the idea of encompassing comprehensive knowledge across all fields of study. Thus, the teachings of life brought by Billy Meier, the Herald of this Universe.

The present moment holds profound significance for embracing broader philosophical or spiritual teachings, such as the Creation Energy Teachings of Billy Meier. These teachings advocate for a deep connection to universal energies and principles, guiding individuals toward a profound understanding of existence and purpose.

The teachings within this book are not my own; I do not profess to be a teacher, nor do I claim such authority. I am merely a student of the Creation Energy Teachings, guided by the wisdom imparted by Billy Meier, the Herald of this Universe. Those seeking better and deeper understanding should seek him. This book only represents my reflections on the knowledge I have acquired through this learning journey.

Following these teachings has become my life's purpose—a steadfast dedication to raising awareness and fostering spiritual growth. It entails living in harmony with natural laws and cosmic energies, nurturing unity and balance in personal and collective endeavors.

In this pursuit, individuals may find fulfillment and purpose by committing themselves to such transformative missions. The aspiration is that by sharing these teachings and insights, others will discover guidance, inspiration, and meaning in their own spiritual journeys.

All the information contained within this book originates from the teachings of the Creation Energy, albeit articulated using different language and expressions.

Ultimately, my hope for the book "NOW," inspired solely by the teachings of Billy Meier, is to catalyze greater awareness, understanding, and positive change in individuals and communities alike. It serves as a catalyst for personal and collective growth, encouraging introspection, dialogue, and proactive steps toward a more harmonious and enlightened world.

Table of Contents

Who is Billy Meier?

As the creation energy teachings stated, Billy is the earthly vessel of Nokodemion, a Spirit whose spiritual journey led him to the Arahat Athersata level, imbuing him with a significant mission.

According to Creational law, the first Spirit to ascend to a purely spiritual level within a Universe assumes the responsibility of teaching its spiritual and Creational laws to its inhabitants.

Throughout Earth's history, Nokodemion has reincarnated multiple times, appearing as prophets and influential figures such as Galileo, Aristotle, Socrates, Mozart, Rasputin, and others.

In religious texts, figures like Henoch, Jeremiah, Isaiah, Elijah, Jmmanuel, aka Jesus Christ, and Mohammed are also manifestations of this Spirit.

In his current incarnation as Billy Meier, Nokodemion continues his role as a Prophet of the New Age, defined as a bringer of truth.

This is his seventh and final incarnation as a Prophet.

After his death, according to the teachings, Nokodemion is expected to reincarnate in 2075 to further the creation energy teachings and will be identified by a birthmark akin to that of Jmmanuel's crucifixion wound.

Nokodemion will remain on Earth until the year 3999, after which he will return to the spiritual realms of Arahat Athersata to continue his spiritual evolution.

Billy thus represents the culmination of Nokodemion's extensive spiritual teachings and prophetic roles throughout history.

His life and teachings play a crucial role in disseminating universal truths and cultivating profound spiritual understanding and harmony among humanity.

The Creation Energy Teaching

Listen, inhabitants of this earthly realm, heed the wisdom of those who guide us—the purveyors of truth, the custodians of spiritual enlightenment, and the stewards of life itself.

According to the teachings, they impart that in the universal order, there exists no beginning or end except for the eternal consciousness that birthed creation and the primal flame from which all emerged and to which all shall return.

Indeed, Billy said everything emanates from a singular essence that transcends form and originates from the formless.

These teachings prompt us to contemplate the profound unity underlying all existence—a unity that surpasses the confines of time and space.

They remind us that our essence is intricately interwoven with the fabric of universal consciousness, intimately linked to the primordial flame that sparks the cosmos.

This understanding challenges us to see beyond illusions of separateness, acknowledging the interconnectedness that binds us together.

Embracing this perspective invites profound insights into reality and our place within it.

It encourages exploration into the depths of consciousness and recognition of the eternal cycle of creation and dissolution.

By honoring the unity amidst diversity, we embark on a journey toward spiritual awareness and a harmonious relationship with the cosmos.

Therefore, let us cherish the teachings of these wise mentors—guides who illuminate the path to understanding our origins, purpose, and interconnected destiny within the vast mosaic of existence.

In doing so, we align ourselves with timeless truths that resonate across cultures and eras, guiding humanity toward a future where unity, wisdom, and spiritual enlightenment prevail.

Spiritual validation transcends the realm of gods

Many people anticipate divine judgment from celestial beings, expecting gods or angelic liberators to appear amidst clouds to adjudicate their fates fairly.

But, according to the teachings of life brought by the Herald, this belief revolves around a dualistic outcome: either consignment to the fiery depths of hell or elevation to heavenly realms among gods and demigods.

However, this awaited scenario remains elusive and improbable. The notion of divine entities passing judgment is rooted in human imagination rather than tangible reality.

Gods and tin gods are perceived constructs devoid of genuine power or existence, existing solely as intangible illusions.

The concept of awaiting divine judgment reveals a profound human desire for justice and validation beyond mortal existence.

It reflects a longing for assurance regarding one's destiny, whether it entails eternal suffering or blissful transcendence.

This belief system hinges on the assumption that supernatural forces govern human destinies, influencing the afterlife based on earthly deeds.

However, the reality posited is starkly different; gods and tin gods are human inventions devoid of substance or agency to oversee mortal affairs.

The dichotomy between hell and paradise, under divine scrutiny, underscores a pervasive cultural narrative rooted in religious teachings and societal norms.

It shapes perceptions of morality and ethical conduct, dictating the parameters for salvation or damnation.

Yet, the certainty of divine intervention remains unsubstantiated.

The purported entities responsible for judgment lack empirical evidence or demonstrable influence over human affairs.

They exist solely within the realm of human belief, serving as symbolic constructs rather than tangible entities capable of influencing cosmic destinies.

The anticipation of divine judgment and the subsequent fate of souls hinges on faith in ethereal beings who are, fundamentally, products of human imagination.

The dichotomy of hell and paradise, presided over by gods and tin gods, represents a narrative framework rather than a factual reality.

This belief underscores humanity's enduring quest for meaning and justice beyond mortal constraints, yet it also highlights the speculative nature of religious constructs.

The quest for spiritual validation transcends the realm of gods and tin gods, residing instead within the depths of human consciousness and societal constructs.

Patience and calmness

Happiness and contentment abound when individuals exhibit gentleness in their demeanor.

As human beings, practicing patience in the midst of challenges and adversity and approaching situations with calmness and rationality is key to maintaining inner peace and promoting harmonious relationships.

According to the teachings, this demeanor reflects an ability to manage emotions such as anger and vengefulness and to align actions with the truths inherent in the laws and recommendations of creation.

Mildness in behavior involves navigating life's complexities with a composed and rational mindset.

It entails approaching conflicts and difficulties with a measured response guided by intellectual discernment and a commitment to uphold ethical principles.

By exercising control over emotions and impulses, individuals can foster an environment conducive to understanding and cooperation.

Patience and calmness in managing situations contribute to personal well-being and interpersonal harmony.

They allow individuals to respond thoughtfully rather than react impulsively, fostering mutual respect and constructive dialogue.

By adhering to the truths embedded in creational laws, individuals promote justice and fairness in their interactions, thereby contributing positively to societal cohesion.

Cultivating mildness in behavior promotes a balanced and fulfilling life.

It enables individuals to navigate challenges with resilience and grace, promoting inner peace and fostering positive relationships with others.

By remembering patience, rationality, and adherence to ethical principles, individuals enhance their own happiness and contribute to a more harmonious and compassionate world.

One's consciousness

Just as a well-furnished, well-ventilated, and harmoniously arranged living space cannot be achieved without careful attention to its arrangement, ventilation, and sunlight, a healthy body and a joyful, radiant face also require a conscious effort.

For these to manifest, one's consciousness must be filled with thoughts of joy, peace, love, and harmony.

Following the teachings, these positive thoughts shape corresponding feelings, which then cultivate goodwill and peaceful cheerfulness in the psyche.

This state of mind, in turn, radiates similar impulses into consciousness, creating a cycle where new, constructive thoughts emerge from this harmonious foundation.

Thus, the consciousness develops in a progressive, life-affirming rhythm, driven by the continuous influence of positive and loving thoughts.

This ongoing development fosters both physical health and a cheerful demeanor, reflecting inner harmony and joy.

In essence, maintaining a positive mental state is crucial for achieving and sustaining a healthy body and a bright, happy face.

Just as a well-maintained living space requires thoughtful care, so too does one's consciousness, which needs nurturing with positive thoughts to achieve overall well-being.

State of connection

Human beings of Earth reflect upon a time when you were free from belief systems that veiled the real truth and were closer to understanding the inherent truths of existence.

It is a call to return to a state where your connection to Creation was rooted not in blind faith or irrational beliefs but in a genuine quest for truth and understanding.

The teachings show this state of being invites you to rediscover the essence of your connection to the universe, untethered from the confines of organized religion and dogma.

In embracing this return to truth, you reclaim a sense of authenticity in your relationship with Creation.

It entails recognizing the natural order and principles that govern the cosmos, acknowledging the interconnectedness of all life forms and the profound wisdom embedded within the fabric of existence.

By relinquishing dependency on external deities and prayers to gods, you align yourself with a deeper understanding of your role as a conscious participant in the cosmic unfolding.

The journey towards reconnecting with truth involves a process of introspection and discernment.

It requires questioning inherited beliefs and societal constructs that may obscure genuine spiritual growth and enlightenment.

By cultivating a direct relationship with Creation based on empirical observation and personal experience, you foster a more profound and meaningful connection to the mysteries of life.

Returning to a state of connection with Creation through truth involves transcending superficial forms of worship or adherence to religious doctrines.

It encourages a reclamation of personal sovereignty and responsibility in navigating the complexities of existence.

By embracing the innate capacity to discern truth from falsehood and to align with universal principles of love, harmony, and compassion, you reclaim agency over your spiritual journey and contribute to a more enlightened and harmonious world.

The call to return to a state of connection with Creation through truth invites human beings to reclaim their innate wisdom and authenticity.

It urges a departure from dogmatic beliefs and organized religion, encouraging a deeper exploration of universal truths and principles that resonate with personal experience and understanding.

By accepting this journey of self-discovery and enlightenment, individuals rediscover their inherent connection to the cosmos and cultivate a more profound sense of purpose and fulfillment in life.

Do not bow to gods of fiction

People of Earth, both men and women, should not kneel before gods.

These deities are fabrications, falsehoods spun by humans who, in their folly, crafted imaginary powers and worshiped them.

Do not follow their lead; do not offer prayers to these invented gods or mimic their actions.

According to Billy, the beliefs in higher beings are mere illusions, products of human imagination, and they do not merit your reverence or devotion.

Instead, embrace your own agency and reason.

Reject the myths and legends that others have constructed.

Seek understanding and truth through rational inquiry and compassion towards your fellow beings.

Humanity's potential lies not in submission to fictitious entities but in the unity and strength derived from collective knowledge and empathy.

By eschewing worship of invented gods, you affirm your commitment to a world shaped by reason, empathy, and the shared human experience.

Let us forge a future where human dignity and progress prevail over superstition and division.

Stand tall as individuals capable of shaping your own destinies and contributing to the greater good.

Respect the diversity of beliefs but hold steadfast to the principles of critical thinking and humanism.

In this way, we can build a society founded on respect for truth, justice, and the inherent worth of every person.

Therefore, do not bow to gods of fiction but stand united in pursuit of a world where humanity's potential is realized through compassion, knowledge, and the shared pursuit of a better future for all.

The delicate balance of life

Human beings, young and old alike, inhabit the vast garden of Earth, partaking in the abundance bestowed upon them by nature, animals, and their own creations.

As the Herald indicated, enjoy the fruits of the land and the nourishment derived from animals and other creatures, ensuring gratitude and moderation in all things.

Savor the fermented juices of fruits in measured quantities, avoiding excess that leads to intoxication.

Similarly, consume the flesh of animals—whether birds, fishes, or mammals like pigs, cattle, and camels—but do so conscientiously, without indulging in gluttony or greed that would lead to wrongdoing.

The teachings invite us to Let the harmony of nature guide our actions, respecting the balance and beauty it offers.

Cherish the sustenance provided by the earth's bounty, mindful of the responsibility to care for it sustainably.

By partaking in food and drink with respect and moderation, we honor the intricate web of life that supports all living beings on this planet.

Strive to cultivate a relationship with the natural world that reflects stewardship and mindfulness.

Adopt the privilege of nourishment from Earth's garden while upholding principles of balance and ethical conduct.

In doing so, we contribute to a world where abundance is shared responsibly, and each individual's actions contribute positively to the collective well-being.

Thus, inhabit Earth's garden with reverence and responsibility, nurturing a harmonious existence that respects the gifts of nature and sustains the delicate balance of life for generations to come.

Dedication to goodness

The teachings tell us to heed this counsel: do not deviate from the path of righteousness when confronted with evil.

To refrain from aiding malevolence in any form, lest you face expulsion from your community and endure ostracism for the remainder of your days.

To hold fast to integrity and moral clarity in all your endeavors.

And resist the allure of wrongdoing and choose instead to uphold justice, kindness, and compassion.

By standing firm against evil, you safeguard not only your own honor but also contribute to the preservation of peace and harmony within your society.

Be vigilant against the temptations that lead you astray.

Remain steadfast in your commitment to principles that uphold dignity and respect for all.

Your actions shape the fabric of your community and define the legacy you leave behind.

Let your choices reflect a steadfast dedication to goodness and truth.

Uphold your responsibilities as stewards of morality and guardians of decency, ensuring that your presence in society remains a beacon of hope and righteousness.

Supernatural virtues

According to the Creation Energy Teachings, there are no supernatural virtues bestowed by imagined deities or gods, as these entities are fictitious and lack the capacity to confer virtues upon individuals.

Instead, virtues must either be inherited in small measure from parents genetically or acquired through personal discipline and self-education by human beings themselves.

As said in the teachings, Human beings do not inherit supernatural virtues from non-existent godheads or other mythical entities.

The notion of divine bestowment of virtues is a product of human imagination rather than a factual reality.

Therefore, any virtues possessed by individuals are either passed down in a limited capacity through genetics from parents or developed through conscious effort and personal growth.

The acquisition of virtues through personal discipline and self-education is integral to human development.

It involves cultivating qualities such as integrity, compassion, courage, and wisdom through deliberate practice and continuous learning.

This process empowers individuals to shape their character and behavior in alignment with ethical principles and societal values, fostering personal growth and contributing positively to their communities.

The idea that supernatural beings endow virtues is a mythological construct.

Billy stated human beings are responsible for their moral and ethical development, which requires dedication, introspection, and a commitment to lifelong learning.

By accepting this responsibility, individuals not only enhance their own character but also contribute to a more compassionate and virtuous society based on reasoned and deliberate ethical choices.

The cycle of existence

Human beings must begin to understand, with truth and logic, that the energy of their creation continues to animate different bodies after each life.

This energy, often referred to as the soul or life force, does not vanish but instead transitions, carrying forward experiences and growth.

Every life serves as a chapter in a continuous journey, where lessons learned contribute to the evolution of the individual spirit.

Understanding this reveals that life and death are not finalities, but parts of an eternal cycle.

In the Universe, nothing truly ceases to exist, rather, everything transforms.

Death is not an end but a pause in which what has been learned is integrated, and what is yet to be experienced awaits.

This mirrors the cycles seen in nature and the cosmos, where growth and rest are interwoven.

The human spirit follows these universal laws, evolving through repeated cycles of life, learning, and rest.

Just as the seasons turn, life and death serve as moments in a larger process of development and renewal.

When a person internalizes this fundamental truth, they are liberated from the need for jealousy, envy, impatience, and deception.

These emotions often stem from a fear of loss or a misunderstanding of life's purpose.

By recognizing that each life contributes to the evolution of their being, people can free themselves from such limiting behaviors.

They understand that no experience, relationship, or possession is permanently lost but part of a larger whole.

Living with this awareness enables individuals to embrace their authentic selves, unburdened by superficial fears or desires.

They can act genuinely, as there is no need to disguise or compete, they are simply part of an ongoing journey.

This is the essence of true freedom, where life is not restricted by temporary gains or losses but is instead a meaningful expression of one's true nature within the larger cycle of existence.

The interconnectedness

The teachings tell us that we should consider that the dwellings of human beings are the Earths, and they are only temporary abodes.

Therefore, it is imperative to make these dwellings beneficial for fellow humans and for the greater good.

Refrain from causing harm or destruction to these earthly habitats.

Strive to enhance the environments where people live, ensuring they are sustainable and nurturing.

Welcome practices that preserve and protect natural resources, promoting a harmonious coexistence with the Earth and its diverse ecosystems.

Recognize all life forms and the responsibility to steward the planet responsibly for future generations.

Let your actions reflect a commitment to sustainability and environmental stewardship.

Support initiatives that promote conservation, mitigate climate impact, and uphold the integrity of ecosystems.

By safeguarding the Earth's habitats, you contribute to a healthier and more resilient planet for all inhabitants.

Regard the Earth as a shared home for humanity and endeavor to leave a positive legacy through actions that promote the well-being of people and the planet.

Reciprocal transfer of energy

In accordance with the teachings, the motion of consciousness, or its swinging wave, is shaped by deliberate efforts in learning and the resulting development or evolution.

This process involves achieving specific goals that consist of various factors that collectively influence and propel the consciousness.

Through this dynamic interaction, energy and power are transmitted from the consciousness to the body.

This exchange is crucial as it sustains the physical and mental engagement necessary for personal growth.

The body, in turn, reciprocates by channeling its energy, power, and endurance back to the consciousness.

This reciprocal transfer of energy and power establishes a continuous loop of influence between the consciousness and the body.

As the consciousness evolves, it drives the body to perform with greater vitality, while the body's energy reinforces the ongoing evolution of consciousness.

Therefore, the growth and movement of consciousness depend significantly on the synergy between mental and physical exertion.

Achieving a balanced and dynamic interaction between these elements ensures that both the body and consciousness are continuously evolving and mutually supporting each other's development.

Application of acquired wisdom

The teachings indicate there are myriad terms and expressions used to describe introspection and self-examination, yet they all ultimately serve the same purpose: to deeply understand oneself—thoughts, emotions, passions, habits, abilities, and potentials.

This introspective journey is not merely about self-analysis for its own sake but aims to uncover the essence of one's being.

It requires utilizing every perception, cognition, and awareness, along with accumulated knowledge, practical experiences, and the wisdom derived from them.

The goal is to align with the ultimate truth—the principles of Creation and its laws and recommendations.

This quest for self-understanding and alignment with universal truths is integral to advancing one's evolution of consciousness.

It goes beyond superficial self-reflection to encompass a comprehensive exploration of one's inner world and external interactions.

By delving into the depths of personal perceptions and experiences, individuals can glean insights that contribute to their spiritual and intellectual growth.

Central to this journey is the application of acquired wisdom and understanding towards living in harmony with the laws of Creation.

These laws provide a framework for ethical conduct, personal development, and interconnectedness with all life forms.

Through diligent application of these principles in daily life, individuals not only deepen their understanding of themselves but also contribute positively to the collective consciousness.

The purpose of introspection and self-examination is to harness every facet of human experience—intellectual, emotional, and spiritual—to uncover fundamental truths and align with universal laws.

This transformative process enables individuals to evolve consciously, contributing meaningfully to their personal growth and the greater good of humanity.

Realistic thoughts

A person experiencing psychic disturbances must learn to liberate themselves from erroneous assumptions, thoughts, and feelings that influence their mental state.

This involves recognizing and relinquishing these misguided beliefs, as well as no longer being swayed by them.

Simultaneously, according to the teachings, it is essential for them to develop new, alternative, and realistic thoughts.

These new thoughts should foster corresponding feelings that positively impact the troubled psyche, offering a constructive way to address and manage their specific issues.

By engaging in this process, individuals can better navigate their problematic situations.

The transition to healthier thoughts and feelings aids in consciously working through challenges and improving their overall mental well-being.

This approach helps individuals address their psychological burdens more effectively and satisfactorily.

Through this mental restructuring, they can achieve greater stability and a more positive outlook on their circumstances.

Internalizing the truth

To overcome feelings of grief, sorrow, unrest, or lovelessness, a person must seek comfort within their own thoughts and the emotions these thoughts produce.

The key lies in directing one's thoughts in a constructive manner so that they align with friendliness, love, and peace.

Achieving this requires a deliberate effort to steer thoughts positively, allowing them to foster a sense of harmony and well-being.

It is not enough to simply hope for change; one must actively shape their thought patterns.

Understanding and embracing the actual truth is crucial in this process.

As stated in the teachings, recognizing the truth brings clarity and enables the development of thoughts that are genuinely peaceful, free, loving, and fulfilling.

The creation of inner peace and emotional well-being hinges on the ability to see, acknowledge, and internalize the truth.

Only by doing so can one transform their thoughts and feelings into sources of comfort and positive change.

The pursuit of excellence

Virtue is not merely a quality but a fundamental capability that allows human beings to manifest the highest expressions of their character.

As the teachings prove, It encompasses a diverse range of attributes that pertain to moral conduct, ethical values, intellectual discernment, wisdom, and the practice of maintaining balance between extremes.

Central to these virtues is genuine love, encompassing compassion and empathy towards others, which holds profound significance in ethical frameworks.

Virtue extends beyond individual traits to encompass a readiness to uphold moral principles in both thought and action.

It involves cultivating a mentality that values integrity, justice, and empathy and translating these values into behaviors that benefit both oneself and society.

This commitment to virtuous living fosters a harmonious relationship between personal conduct and ethical standards, contributing to a more just and compassionate community.

At its core, virtue embodies the pursuit of excellence in character and behavior.

It encourages individuals to cultivate moral clarity and resilience, enabling them to navigate complex ethical dilemmas with integrity and wisdom.

By adhering to the principle of finding a rightful middle ground between extremes, individuals demonstrate their commitment to fairness, moderation, and ethical balance in all aspects of life.

Ultimately, the practice of virtue serves as a cornerstone for personal growth and societal harmony.

It empowers individuals to embody principles of truth, justice, and compassion, fostering a community where ethical behavior is not just valued but actively pursued.

Through the cultivation of virtues, human beings enrich their own lives and contribute positively to the collective well-being of humanity.

One's mental outlook

Based on the teachings, there is no better healer for a person than their own healthy, fresh, pure, and neutral-positive thoughts.

This is especially true for the psyche, which is profoundly affected by the nature of thoughts that shape its state through feelings.

Positive and harmonious thoughts foster a peaceful and balanced mental state, which can significantly impact overall well-being.

Thoughts also influence physical illnesses to a degree, as their power can aid in the healing process.

While thoughts alone do not have absolute control over physical ailments—often requiring medical treatments or surgeries—they still play a crucial role in the patient's attitude toward their illness.

A person's mental response to their condition greatly affects their mood and, consequently, the healing process.

If a person's attitude, mood, or disposition towards their illness is negative or pessimistic, it can hinder and delay healing.

Conversely, a positive and constructive attitude can enhance and expedite the healing process.

The overall impact of thoughts on healing is evident, though the treatability of the illness remains a critical factor.

In some cases, even with illnesses deemed incurable, positive and constructive thoughts have led to surprising recoveries.

This demonstrates that the power of thought can be a decisive factor in overcoming challenges, proving that the strength of one's mental outlook can indeed influence the outcome of one's health.

Creation

Creation is the singular presence, power, and source of all existence.

It stands alone in the universe, with no competitors or realities outside of it.

Omnipotent, omniscient, and omnipresent, Creation is the essence of everything that exists, and nothing can exist without it.

The universal consciousness of Creation is a natural outcome of its own evolution, and like all living beings, it adheres to the creational-natural laws.

This pure spirit-energy form of Creation exists on a plane so far beyond the material that it is impossible for it to communicate directly with human beings.

Creation is a single, independent form of energy, not defined by dualities or trinities, nor by human characteristics like gender or personality.

It is a constantly evolving force, neither good nor evil, but perfectly balanced.

In this neutral state, everything that exists follows the same laws, and life forms, including humans, develop qualities such as good or evil only through experiences.

Creation is not a parental figure, and while we often use familial terms to describe our relationship with it, these are simply metaphors to help us understand its vastness.

Humans often refer to themselves as children of "God," but this concept is a misunderstanding.

"God" is a title particularly associated with the JHWH, a king of wisdom in ancient Lyran-descended societies.

The gods of the Earth were human being extraterrestrials.

Creation transcends all titles, hierarchies, or names, and though we might use terms like "The Force" or "The One" to describe it, none fully capture its essence.

Creation is both far beyond our comprehension and as close to us as our own breath. The only true separation from Creation is an illusion born from our own beliefs.

Belief in Creation is not necessary for its existence, as Creation does not depend on our faith.

Instead, it is we who are affected by our understanding of Creation.

Creation is not bound to any religion, but all religions exist within the vastness of Creation.

There are no chosen people or specific ways to comprehend Creation, as we are all equally connected to it.

Each of us is a "divine son" of Creation, part of its infinite nature, exploring the endless wonders of existence.

Within each person, a spark of Creation resides, connecting us eternally to the whole.

This connection is unbreakable, ensuring that we are always a part of Creation.

Recognizing this connection fills us with immense joy, for it highlights our role as co-creators with Creation.

In embracing our greatness and specialness as beings of Creation, we are engulfed by the overwhelming love and splendor of this infinite and all-encompassing force.

The natural laws of Creation

The natural laws of Creation embody principles that, when followed and applied, bring about beneficial effects.

Adhering to these laws leads to prosperity, success, joy, love, peace, harmony, and wisdom.

By aligning with these inherent principles, individuals and societies can experience abundance and fulfillment.

According to the teachings, these laws promote balance, fairness, and sustainability in all aspects of life.

Holding them fosters harmonious relationships, both with oneself and with others, cultivating a sense of unity and interconnectedness.

Furthermore, living in accordance with these natural laws enhances clarity and insight, guiding decisions and actions towards positive outcomes.

They serve as guiding beacons that illuminate pathways toward personal growth, communal well-being, and a harmonious existence with the environment.

In essence, the wisdom inherent in these natural laws offers a framework for living that nurtures holistic prosperity and contributes to a world where happiness, peace, and fulfillment are attainable for all.

Nature commune

The teachings advise everyone to venture into the open expanse of nature to discern its laws and to heed its guidance.

By doing so, the fear of death can be dispelled, and one can face the end of this present existence without regret or foolishness.

Nature reveals profound truths and rhythms that govern life's cycles.

By immersing oneself in its beauty and observing its processes, one can gain a deeper understanding of life and its impermanence.

This understanding fosters acceptance and equanimity, freeing individuals from the grip of fear and sorrow.

Embracing nature's teachings enables a harmonious alignment with the natural order, promoting a sense of connection and purpose.

It encourages living in accordance with principles that honor life and contribute positively to the world.

By recognizing and respecting nature's laws, individuals cultivate resilience and wisdom that transcend the boundaries of mortal existence.

Therefore, commune with nature to discover its timeless wisdom, allowing it to illuminate the path towards a life lived fully and without fear, preparing for transitions with grace and understanding.

The wisdom of nature

According to the spiritual teachings, choosing to remain ignorant and dismissing the wonders of nature, as well as the laws bestowed by Creation and natural formation, is self-destructive.

It leads to a life filled with false peace, illusory freedom, and counterfeit love, steeped in ignorance, lack of wisdom, joylessness, and disharmony.

Consequently, this obstructs the evolution of your inner world, causing stagnation.

Refusing to acknowledge the profound lessons and laws inherent in nature denies oneself the opportunity for growth and understanding.

It perpetuates a state of confusion and disconnection from the true essence of existence.

By disregarding these foundational truths, individuals deprive themselves of genuine fulfillment and meaningful progress in their personal development.

Embracing the wisdom of nature and the laws of Creation fosters a deeper connection with oneself and the world.

It nurtures inner growth, clarity, and harmony, paving the way for a life enriched by genuine peace, authentic freedom, and profound love.

It is through this alignment with natural principles that individuals can experience true evolution and fulfillment of consciousness.

Therefore, recognize the profound truths present in nature and honor the laws of Creation.

Welcome knowledge and wisdom, cultivate joy and harmony, and embark on a journey of inner growth that propels you forward in life's journey.

Laws and guidelines

People of Earth, in accordance with the creation energy teachings, learn to contemplate the boundless goodness of life and the benevolent deeds that have been bestowed upon you since time immemorial, meant for all who adhere to the natural and creational laws and principles.

Throughout history, those who have aligned themselves with these inherent laws and guidelines have reaped the benefits of a harmonious existence.

They have experienced the rewards of living in harmony with nature, enjoying its abundance and nurturing its delicate balance.

By respecting these principles, they have found fulfillment and purpose in their lives, contributing positively to their communities and the world at large.

Reflect upon the enduring legacy of those who have walked the path guided by these natural and creational laws.

Their actions have fostered peace, compassion, and unity among humanity, embodying the essence of goodness and righteousness.

Their example inspires others to follow in their footsteps, creating a ripple effect of positivity and transformation.

As you ponder the unceasing generosity of life and the opportunities it presents, consider embracing these laws and guidelines.

Let them guide your actions and decisions, leading you toward a life of meaning, abundance, and fulfillment.

In doing so, you honor the legacy of those who have come before you and pave the way for a future where goodness and harmony prevail for all.

Fruitless introspection

Following the creation energy teachings, in essence, stability in one's existence hinges upon the continual pursuit of goodness and positivity in every facet of life.

There is no enduring foundation without this perpetual motion toward the positive. Reflecting on ancestral legacy offers little solace, as historical blindness exists then as it does now.

Each individual must first illuminate their own path and refine their being, as personal transformation is paramount.

Neither spouse can solely affect the other, nor can parents or children solely influence their kin.

Each person bears their own responsibility and must act independently to shape their present reality.

Pondering over these truths and one's own circumstances yields no tangible benefits.

It is crucial to acknowledge that all is anchored in the creational laws, aligning with the strengths of character and virtues inherent in universal consciousness.

Every life form, without exception, possesses equal rights and corresponding responsibilities.

Instead of fruitless introspection, individuals are urged to embrace the immutable truths predefined by Creation and its laws.

The key lies not in futile contemplation but in embracing these foundational truths that resonate through the universe's design.

Each individual's journey toward fulfillment and stability is guided by these universal principles, emphasizing personal accountability and the pursuit of positive transformation.

Inherent potential

Every human being is endowed with innate gifts bestowed by the laws and recommendations of Creation.

The teachings stated that these gifts encompass the physical faculties, the capacity for rational thought, and the profound discernment of consciousness.

Through these endowments, individuals possess the ability to perceive, reason, and comprehend the complexities of existence.

The powers of the body enable individuals to engage with the physical world, harnessing strength, agility, and resilience to navigate life's challenges.

These gifts facilitate actions that sustain life, promote health, and contribute to personal well-being.

Cognition, or rationality, empowers individuals to analyze information, solve problems, and make informed decisions.

It serves as a guiding force in understanding cause and effect, fostering learning and adaptation to changing circumstances.

True discernment, rooted in intellect and consciousness, allows individuals to explore deeper meanings and insights beyond surface appearances.

It involves introspection, moral reasoning, and the ability to discern between right and wrong, guiding ethical conduct and moral choices.

Collectively, these natural gifts provide a foundation for human potential and growth.

They equip individuals with the tools necessary to cultivate personal development, foster meaningful relationships, and contribute positively to society.

By accepting and honing these gifts, individuals fulfill their inherent potential and contribute to a world enriched by knowledge, compassion, and ethical awareness.

The laws and recommendations of Creation

According to the Herald, the laws and recommendations set forth by Creation are designed to guide humanity towards the pursuit of true love, knowledge, wisdom, and moral excellence.

These principles form a framework that encourages individuals to cultivate compassion, empathy, and genuine care for others, fostering harmonious relationships and collective well-being.

Striving towards true love involves not only compassion towards others but also selflessness and empathy.

By embracing these principles, individuals contribute to a world where kindness and understanding prevail, nurturing a sense of community and unity.

The pursuit of knowledge and wisdom is another cornerstone of the laws of Creation.

It encourages continuous learning, critical thinking, and intellectual growth.

By seeking knowledge, individuals expand their understanding of the world and their place within it, gaining insights that inform ethical decision-making and responsible actions.

Furthermore, the laws of Creation emphasize the importance of moral and virtuous perfection.

This entails upholding principles of integrity, honesty, and fairness in all aspects of life.

By adhering to these values, individuals strive towards personal growth and contribute positively to societal progress, fostering a culture of respect and dignity.

In essence, the laws and recommendations of Creation provide a blueprint for living a meaningful and purposeful life.

They guide individuals towards embracing love, pursuing knowledge and wisdom, and embodying moral and virtuous excellence.

By adhering to these principles, individuals contribute to a more compassionate, enlightened, and harmonious world.

Selfishness

A selfish person often fails to recognize that their psychological conflicts, suffering, and injuries are self-created, not the responsibility of others.

Instead of understanding this, they project their issues onto those around them, leading them to harbor hatred and act against others.

According to the teachings, this behavior manifests as attempts to moralize, persuade, manipulate, or dominate, aiming to control others and alleviate their own psychological distress.

In their quest to manage their own suffering and insecurity, these individuals might resort to controlling behaviors to maintain a sense of power and independence.

Their selfish desire for possessions, profit, and wealth further drives them to exert control over others, believing that such dominance will alleviate their own internal conflicts.

As they accumulate wealth, power, or a higher worldly position, their desire for control can intensify.

This can evolve into an unhealthy obsession with domination, where the pursuit of absolute authority becomes paramount.

The individual's need to exert power often reflects a deeper insecurity and inability to address their own issues.

The selfish person's actions are a reflection of their own unresolved psychological conflicts.

Their attempts to dominate and manipulate others are not only driven by personal insecurity but also by a relentless pursuit of material gain and control.

This behavior underscores their failure to understand that the true resolution of their inner turmoil cannot come from controlling others but must be addressed within themselves.

Cultivating knowledge

Those lacking knowledge of the truth resemble worthless chaff, easily scattered by the wind.

Undoubtedly, according to the teachings, their actions lack substance and significance, akin to weightless husks separated from valuable grain.

Their words, fleeting and insubstantial like mist and smoke, carry no lasting impact or influence.

Like chaff blown aimlessly by the wind, those without an understanding of truth are adrift in uncertainty and insignificance.

Their endeavors lack purpose and fail to contribute meaningfully to the greater good.

Without a foundation rooted in truth and wisdom, their efforts dissipate into obscurity, leaving no enduring legacy or impact.

In contrast, knowledge of the truth imbues actions with purpose and integrity.

Understanding and adhering to principles of truthfulness and wisdom empower individuals to make meaningful contributions to society.

Their words carry weight and authority, resonating with clarity and purpose to inspire positive change and progress.

Welcoming the truth elevates individuals beyond fleeting uncertainties and superficiality.

It fosters clarity of purpose and a commitment to values that endure.

By cultivating knowledge and understanding of truth, individuals enrich their lives and the lives of others, ensuring that their actions and words resonate with authenticity and lasting significance.

The eternal cycle

Life is an eternal continuum, encompassing the essence of existence in all its forms.

The creative energy that resides within humans, animals, and plants is the very essence of life, animating and sustaining all living things.

This energy creates a profound connection between every part of the natural world, uniting them in a shared experience of existence.

Death should be viewed not as an end but as a natural counterpart to birth, representing two sides of the same coin known as life.

While birth marks the beginning of our journey, death signifies a transition and a return to the cycle that perpetuates life.

This cyclical nature highlights the continuity of life rather than its cessation.

Reincarnation is a fundamental aspect of this eternal cycle, representing the process by which life renews itself.

The law of reincarnation states that life does not simply end with death but transforms and continues in different forms.

This truth can profoundly influence how we view our existence, reducing the fear of death and encouraging us to embrace life more fully.

Understanding our place in the continuous flow of life allows us to see ourselves as part of a larger, enduring lineage.

By recognizing that we have lived and died countless times, we can alleviate existential anxieties and live more freely, unburdened by the fear of the unknown.

This awareness connects us with the legacy of our ancestors and helps us appreciate our role in the ongoing cycle of existence.

Decaying wood

Following the teachings, many among you revel in megalomania and selfishness, striving to bask in the spotlight of your peers and gain their admiration.

This pursuit often originates from a corrupted nature and a troubled psyche, driven by a deep-seated desire to outshine others.

These efforts are steeped in immodesty and a relentless quest for personal validation, leading to an existence devoid of true joy and fairness.

Your happiness becomes as fragile as decaying wood, and your actions are akin to the futile decay of rotting fruit.

The fixation on self-promotion and the allure of public attention can distort your true nature and inner peace.

By placing undue emphasis on outward appearances and the perceptions of others, you risk losing sight of genuine fulfillment and lasting contentment.

The relentless pursuit of recognition leaves many spiritually bankrupt, as the pursuit of superficial achievements fails to nourish deeper emotional needs.

In this pursuit, there lies a fundamental contradiction: while you strive to project an image of happiness and success, your inner world often remains fraught with turmoil and dissatisfaction.

The fleeting nature of your happiness mirrors the fragile state of decaying wood, susceptible to collapse under the weight of reality.

Your actions, driven by selfish desires and a craving for validation, bear little fruit of lasting value, resembling the insignificance of decaying and rotting fruit.

The path of self-centeredness and vanity proves unsustainable, offering only a fleeting facade of happiness and fulfillment.

The pursuit of superficial acclaim and attention, rooted in ego and self-interest, masks a deeper yearning for genuine connection and purpose.

Until this inner conflict is resolved, you risk perpetuating a cycle of dissatisfaction and spiritual emptiness, your life paralleling the transient existence of decaying wood and rotting fruit.

Controlling your thoughts

Controlling your thoughts is key to managing your actions and, thus, your life.

Your thoughts directly influence how you behave and make decisions, so by mastering them, you take charge of your life's direction and outcomes.

You are fundamentally the architect of your own life, a role that has always belonged to you and will continue to do so.

The responsibility for shaping your life rests entirely with you.

By understanding and embracing this role, you gain the power to make deliberate choices that align with your goals and values.

Steering your thoughts in a purposeful manner allows you to create actions that reflect your true intentions.

In summary, the ability to control your thoughts is crucial for controlling your actions and shaping your life.

Acknowledge your role as the architect of your existence, and use this power to construct a life that embodies your aspirations and desires.

Like a tree

Embody the truth as steadfastly as a tree planted beside streams of water, which flourishes and yields abundant, nourishing fruits.

Just as such a tree maintains its vitality with leaves that remain vibrant and unwithered, so too should you uphold the principles of truth and integrity in every aspect of your life.

Doubtlessly, the teachings say that being rooted in truth means aligning your actions and beliefs with honesty, authenticity, and moral principles.

Like the tree sustained by the nourishing waters, embracing truth provides a foundation for personal growth and resilience in the face of challenges.

Strive to bear "good fruits" in your endeavors, contributing positively to your community and the world around you.

These fruits symbolize the outcomes of your actions—whether they are acts of kindness, wisdom, or compassion—that enrich the lives of others and reflect your commitment to living in harmony with truth.

Just as a tree's leaves remain vibrant and healthy, let your adherence to truth sustain your inner well-being and moral clarity.

Upholding integrity in all circumstances ensures that you remain grounded in values that promote justice, empathy, and respect for others.

In essence, being like a tree planted by streams of water signifies a life guided by truth and nourished by ethical principles.

By embodying these qualities, you contribute to a world where authenticity, compassion, and moral integrity flourish, enriching both your own existence and the lives of those around you.

The pursuit of knowledge

According to Billy, the pursuit of knowledge necessitates both discipline and expansion, requiring individuals to harness their understanding through diligent study and application.

By adhering to the laws of nature and the principles of Creation, one can cultivate a profound comprehension of the universe's workings.

This pursuit extends beyond mere acquisition to encompass a holistic integration of knowledge enriched by personal insights and experiences.

Through disciplined study and contemplation of natural laws and primal principles, individuals embark on a journey of self-discovery and enlightenment.

This process involves exploring the interconnectedness of all phenomena and uncovering the underlying patterns that govern existence.

By delving into these principles, individuals not only deepen their understanding of the world but also cultivate a sense of reverence and respect for the intricate balance of nature.

The quest for knowledge is not solely intellectual but also spiritual and emotional, encompassing the pursuit of love, freedom, peace, harmony, and wisdom.

These qualities form the essence of a well-rounded and enlightened individual, embodying virtues that transcend mere factual knowledge.

By integrating these principles into their lives, individuals strive towards becoming embodiments of wisdom and compassion, capable of fostering positive change within themselves and their communities.

The journey toward becoming relatively all-knowing and wise is a lifelong endeavor rooted in continuous growth and self-improvement.

It requires individuals to remain open to new ideas, perspectives, and experiences, embracing the diversity of knowledge that enriches their understanding of the world.

Through their efforts to integrate and apply this knowledge, individuals contribute to the collective evolution of humanity, embodying the principles of love, freedom, peace, harmony, and wisdom in their daily lives.

The pursuit of knowledge through disciplined study and contemplation of natural laws and primal principles leads to a profound understanding of the universe and oneself.

By embodying virtues such as love, freedom, peace, harmony, and wisdom, individuals not only expand their intellectual horizons but also cultivate a deeper sense of purpose and fulfillment.

Through continuous learning and personal growth, individuals contribute to the betterment of society, enriching the world with their insights and compassion.

Depraved thoughts

According to the creation energy teachings, when thoughts are depraved, this degradation inevitably affects one's life and body, as the power of thought dictates the outcomes it produces.

The quality of thoughts is fundamental, as they serve as the source from which actions, life experiences, and personal fulfillment arise.

If the originating thoughts are negative, the resulting actions, life circumstances, and associated factors will also be negative.

As long as a person harbors unclean, pessimistic, wrong, sick, or negative thoughts, their feelings will correspondingly shape their psyche, which in turn influences both their life and physical health.

Negative thoughts will manifest in similarly negative feelings and a compromised state of being, reflecting their detrimental impact on overall well-being.

Conversely, if the thoughts are pure, positive, and constructive, they will lead to beneficial actions and improved life circumstances.

Positive thoughts foster a healthier, more fulfilling life, influencing both actions and external conditions in a favorable way.

The nature of one's thoughts profoundly impacts one's feelings, psyche, and overall life situation.

Positive and pure thoughts lead to constructive outcomes, while negative and depraved thoughts result in adverse effects. Thus, the quality of thought plays a crucial role in shaping one's life and health.

Armed with this knowledge

The teachings point out that those who possess true knowledge and wisdom, regardless of their race or background, understand the fundamental truth of creation and its formation.

Their profound understanding of these principles allows them to navigate life with clarity and purpose, embracing the inherent wisdom that transcends cultural and societal boundaries.

Through this knowledge, they find themselves aligned with the cosmic truths that govern existence, paving the way for them to receive just rewards throughout their lifetimes.

The wisdom of understanding creation's truths empowers individuals to live fearlessly and without sorrow.

Armed with this knowledge, they navigate life's challenges with resilience and inner peace, knowing that their actions are in harmony with the universal order.

This sense of alignment with truth and creation shields them from the uncertainties and anxieties that often plague others, allowing them to experience life fully and authentically.

In embracing the truth of creation, individuals of all backgrounds and beliefs find a common ground—a shared understanding that transcends differences and fosters unity.

This unity is rooted in the recognition of universal principles that govern the cosmos, guiding humanity toward collective evolution and harmony.

Those who embrace this truth cultivate a sense of interconnectedness with all life, fostering compassion, empathy, and mutual respect across diverse communities.

The rewards bestowed upon those who stand in knowledge of creation's truths extend beyond material gains or recognition.

They experience a profound sense of fulfillment and purpose, knowing that their lives are guided by principles that uphold justice, truth, and harmony.

This inner peace and contentment enable them to contribute positively to their communities and the world at large, embodying the essence of wisdom and enlightenment that transcends individual circumstances.

Therefore, those who possess true knowledge and understanding of creation's truths are endowed with a life free from fear and sorrow.

Their alignment with universal principles empowers them to navigate life's complexities with clarity and resilience, fostering unity and harmony across diverse cultures and beliefs.

By accepting these truths, individuals unlock the keys to a meaningful existence, guided by principles that uphold justice, compassion, and the interconnectedness of all life.

True prophets

In accordance with the teachings, we should listen attentively to the words of wisdom imparted by true prophets, for their guidance holds the key to your well-being and prosperity.

Their teachings are grounded in timeless truths that illuminate the path toward inner peace, harmony, and fulfillment.

True prophets offer insights that resonate with the core principles of justice, compassion, and spiritual enlightenment.

By embracing their wisdom, you gain clarity and direction in navigating life's challenges and opportunities.

Their words serve as a compass, guiding you towards actions that align with moral integrity and societal harmony.

To heed the words of true prophets is to prioritize ethical conduct and conscientious living.

Their teachings inspire introspection and self-improvement, encouraging you to cultivate virtues such as empathy, humility, and resilience.

By internalizing their messages, you empower yourself to make informed decisions that contribute positively to your personal growth and the greater good.

Indeed, grasping the wisdom of true prophets fosters a deeper connection to spiritual truths and universal principles.

Their guidance offers solace in times of uncertainty and inspires courage to confront adversity with grace and wisdom.

By following their teachings, you embark on a transformative journey toward a life filled with meaning, purpose, and profound inner fulfillment.

The cycle of stagnation

According to the teachings, among your ranks, there are many who do not harness their thoughts and emotions in a constructive and evolutionary manner.

Instead, these internal processes often degrade into aimless rumination.

Some among you mistakenly dwell in remorse and humility, hoping to uncover past errors and strategize ways to avoid repeating them.

However, this approach yields little progress, as perpetual rumination rarely leads to actionable solutions or definitive resolutions.

The cycle of rumination tends to perpetuate itself without clear outcomes or advancement.

It becomes a stagnant loop where thoughts circle endlessly without fruitful conclusions.

This mental state of constant reflection without proactive steps forward impedes personal growth and obstructs the path to greater understanding and enlightenment.

True evolution of consciousness requires more than passive introspection or dwelling on past mistakes.

It demands a proactive engagement with one's thoughts and emotions, using them as tools for growth and transformation.

Rather than getting lost in remorseful thoughts, individuals are encouraged to channel their reflections towards constructive actions and positive changes in behavior.

Thus, the challenge lies not in dwelling on past shortcomings but in using introspection as a springboard for personal development.

By shifting focus from mere rumination to purposeful reflection and active change, individuals can break free from the cycle of stagnation and embark on a journey towards genuine evolution of consciousness.

The creative force

The creative force, Creation, stands alone as the originator of everything present on Earth and throughout the vast expanse of the universe.

According to Billy, It is through this creative power that all life and existence have come into being, meticulously crafted and perfected according to its logical principles rooted in truth.

These principles serve as the foundational framework that governs the unfolding of life in its myriad forms, shaping the very essence of existence itself.

Within each individual and every life form, the creative force manifests as the breath of life—a vital component intricately woven into the fabric of being.

This essence not only sustains but also animates and connects all living entities, transcending physical boundaries to encompass the spiritual and metaphysical dimensions of existence.

It is through this intrinsic connection to the creative force that life finds its unity and purpose, harmonizing with the larger cosmic order.

The logical principles inherent in Creation guide the evolution and development of life, fostering growth, diversity, and interconnectedness across all realms of existence.

From the smallest microorganisms to the grandest galaxies, each entity embodies a unique expression of the creative force's wisdom and intention.

This universal coherence underscores the profound interdependence and unity that permeate the entirety of creation, reinforcing the intrinsic value and significance of every living being.

Recognizing the creative force as the source of all life and existence invites individuals to embrace a deeper understanding of their place within the cosmos.

It encourages reverence for the interconnected web of life and an appreciation for the diversity and complexity that characterize existence.

By acknowledging the creative force's role in shaping reality through its logical and truthful principles, individuals can align themselves with the greater purpose of contributing positively to the ongoing evolution and harmony of the universe.

The creative force, or Creation, stands as the singular entity responsible for the inception and completion of all life and existence within the universe.

Its logical principles, rooted in truth, serve as the guiding foundation that shapes the intricate tapestry of reality.

Nurturing the creative force's presence within oneself and all living beings fosters a profound sense of interconnectedness and reverence for the sanctity of life.

It is through this recognition and alignment with the principles of Creation that individuals can find fulfillment and meaning in their journey through existence, contributing harmoniously to the cosmic dance of creation and evolution.

On the 21st day

As detailed in the creation energy teachings, the animation of the fetus begins on the 21st day after conception when the spirit-form becomes active.

This marks the start of the individual's existence, as the spirit-form's rebirth or reincarnation within the fetus coincides with the initiation of the heart's rhythmic activity.

At this moment, the new personality and the entire consciousness block are brought into new life.

Prior to this critical moment, there are various processes occurring within the fertilized egg, typically up to around the 14th day after conception.

These processes can include events such as the division into twins.

These early stages are crucial as they lay the groundwork for the later development of the fetus.

During this initial period, the fertilized egg undergoes significant transformations that are essential for proper development.

The formation and separation of cells set the stage for the more complex processes that follow.

The transition into the 21st day signifies the beginning of individual existence, marked by the spirit-form's activity and the onset of the heart's rhythm.

This moment is pivotal, as it represents the convergence of spiritual and physical development, resulting in the birth of a new personality and consciousness.

Greater fulfillment

Those who, in the midst of distress, grief, sorrow, unrest, lovelessness, and misery, recognize and embrace the truth, love, effective peace, and genuine inner freedom will find victory over their own negative states and thoughts.

In accordance with the teachings, by aligning their thoughts with these positive values, they achieve mastery over themselves and their emotional turmoil.

In contrast, individuals who continually harbor thoughts of negativity, malice, selfishness, egotism, mistrust, envy, cynicism, and other detrimental attitudes imprison themselves within self-created confinement.

Such negative thinking binds them and restricts their personal growth and freedom.

Conversely, those who focus on nurturing thoughts that are good, right, positive, peaceful, joyful, and harmonious while maintaining a friendly attitude toward others will experience an abundance of peace, love, joy, and harmony in their own lives.

As the Herald stated, this positive mindset attracts similar values and enriches their existence.

By diligently pursuing truth, knowledge, and wisdom and seeking the good and positive aspects in all life situations and experiences, individuals cultivate altruistic qualities.

This approach opens them to greater fulfillment and aligns them with the abundance of peace, love, and joy, ultimately benefiting themselves and those around them.

Neutrality

In line with the teachings, neutrality, often discussed theoretically, reveals a stark contrast between theory and practice. Delving deeply into this concept unveils that applied neutrality significantly simplifies daily life.

Practicing neutral-positive thinking and behavior forms the foundation for a successful, happy, peaceful, and harmonious life.

However, understanding what lived neutrality truly requires meticulous exploration and engagement with its intricacies.

Mastery of neutral-positive thinking aligns with universal laws, empowering individuals to embrace self-responsibility consciously.

In discussions on neutrality, its practical implications are frequently overshadowed by its theoretical nature.

Only through detailed examination does one comprehend the depth of neutrality's demands and the underlying principles it embodies.

Learning to think neutrally and positively is integral to spiritual growth and personal evolution.

Neglecting this essential aspect in spiritual studies while focusing solely on physical and scientific laws undermines holistic development.

Neutrality cannot be adopted effortlessly at will; it demands significant effort and dedication. From a young age, individuals are conditioned to perceive reality through subjective lenses shaped by thoughts, feelings, assumptions, prejudices, and judgments.

Unlearning these biases and cultivating neutral-objectivity is a transformative process that requires persistence and commitment.

Therefore, integrating neutral-positive thinking into daily life involves a deliberate and ongoing effort to align with the laws of creation and fulfill one's evolutionary potential.

The human body

According to the teachings, the human body is animated by the spirit, which, as a minute fragment of Creation, represents the true essence of life.

This spirit is not just the principle that enlivens the body, but it also encompasses and retains the essence of genuine evolution.

This evolution occurs both consciously and unconsciously, influenced by the material consciousness and the overall consciousness block.

The spirit acts as the driving force behind life and evolution, operating in alignment with creational laws and principles.

It channels the power of striving through the material consciousness, which independently functions and evolves through its own world of thoughts.

The body's role is to serve as the expression medium for this material consciousness.

Thus, the body follows the directives and processes dictated by the material consciousness. These processes may manifest either consciously and deliberately or unconsciously and automatically.

The body's reactions and behaviors are thus reflections of the material consciousness's influence.

While the spirit enlivens the body and harbors the true essence of evolution, the body itself acts as the expression of the material consciousness.

This dynamic interplay highlights how the spirit and consciousness together shape the human experience and development.

Butterfly

Helping a butterfly out of its cocoon often ends up causing more harm than good.

The process of emerging from the cocoon is a critical part of the butterfly's development, allowing it to strengthen its wings and prepare for life outside.

By intervening, one might disrupt this essential process, ultimately jeopardizing the butterfly's survival.

Similarly, attempting to force a bud out of a seed can destroy it.

The natural growth process of a seed requires time and the proper conditions to nurture a bud into a flower.

Rushing this process or applying external pressure can damage the seedling and prevent it from growing correctly.

This principle extends to the realm of human consciousness.

Trying to awaken someone who is not yet ready can lead to confusion rather than genuine understanding.

Personal growth and awareness are processes that need to unfold naturally and cannot be artificially accelerated.

Certain developmental processes cannot be rushed or manipulated from the outside.

They require a natural progression to ensure proper growth and transformation.

External interference often disrupts the necessary balance for successful development.

Meaningful progress and growth must come from within, as some transformations cannot be facilitated externally.

Respecting the natural course of development and allowing processes to unfold on their own are crucial for achieving authentic and lasting change.

Constructive mindset

In line with the teachings, anxious thoughts have a profoundly demoralizing impact on various aspects of life, including feelings, psyche, morale, mood, and overall personality.

These negative thoughts can also affect physical health, life circumstances, and one's environment.

Over time, harmful and incorrect thoughts can destabilize the entire nervous system, even if they are not physically expressed.

In contrast, thoughts that are strong, pure, balanced, healthy, and positive build vitality and resilience against negativity and destruction.

Such thoughts contribute to the protection and well-being of the body, which is highly sensitive and responsive to the nature of the thoughts one harbors.

This underscores the importance of maintaining a positive and constructive mental attitude.

Habitual negative thinking can lead to severe adverse effects, both physically and mentally.

Therefore, it is crucial to cultivate a thinking process that is constructive, progressive, and renewing.

This approach ensures that the power of thoughts is directed towards achieving beneficial and aspirational goals.

The nature of one's thoughts has a significant impact on health and overall life circumstances.

By fostering a positive and constructive mindset, individuals can enhance their well-being and effectively counteract negative influences.

Thus, it is essential to consciously manage thoughts to achieve beneficial outcomes for oneself and one's environment.

The denial of Creation and its guiding principles

From the creation energy teachings, we learn that Creation encompasses not only the physical universe but also the spiritual and metaphysical dimensions that permeate existence.

It represents the underlying order and purpose that governs the cosmos, offering insights into the interconnectedness of all living beings.

The principles inherent in Creation serve as guiding beacons, illuminating paths of understanding and fostering unity among diverse forms of life.

Life itself is a testament to the profound interplay between Creation's principles of love and truth.

Every being experiences cycles of existence, marked by periods of growth, transformation, and renewal.

These cycles are not merely physical but also spiritual, offering opportunities for learning, evolution, and the eventual attainment of unity with the creative force.

Through these experiences, individuals and life forms contribute to the unfolding tapestry of existence, each playing a unique role in the greater cosmic symphony.

The denial of Creation and its guiding principles hinders the recognition of life's intrinsic purpose and interconnectedness.

It disregards the profound journey of self-discovery and spiritual growth that each soul embarks upon. Embracing the existence of Creation invites individuals to align themselves with universal truths of love, compassion, and harmony, fostering a deeper understanding of their roles within the grand design of existence.

It is through this alignment that life finds fulfillment and meaning, transcending individual experiences to contribute harmoniously to the greater whole.

The acknowledgment of Creation and its inherent truths—rooted in love, truth, and the cycles of life and rebirth—offers a profound perspective on the interconnectedness and purpose of existence.

It underscores the transformative journey that all life embarks upon, each contributing uniquely to the ongoing evolution of consciousness.

By honoring the principles of Creation, individuals embrace a path of enlightenment and unity, aligning themselves with the cosmic dance of creation and renewal that defines the essence of existence itself.

Do not be swayed

Turn your gaze away from the actions of the irresponsible and conscienceless, for their deeds offer fleeting enjoyment and ultimately lead to their own sorrow.

Undeniably, the teachings tell us to resist the temptation to follow their path, as it is one of temporary gratification and eventual regret.

The actions of the unfair and unrighteous may seem enticing in the moment, but they are unsustainable and devoid of lasting fulfillment.

By refusing to emulate their behavior, you uphold principles of integrity and moral responsibility, safeguarding your own well-being and moral compass.

Instead, focus on pursuing actions that align with fairness and righteousness.

Choose paths that contribute positively to your own growth and the well-being of others.

By adhering to these principles, you cultivate a sense of purpose and inner peace that transcends temporary pleasures.

Remember that true fulfillment arises from living authentically and ethically.

By remaining steadfast in your commitment to fairness and righteousness, you set an example for others and contribute to a more just and harmonious society.

Let your actions reflect your values, and do not be swayed by the allure of short-lived gains at the expense of long-term integrity.

A time will come

A time will come when humanity will recognize the beauty and freedom of living a simple life.

As people begin to detach from the distractions of materialism and excess, they will find a deeper appreciation for the peace and fulfillment that simplicity brings.

This shift in consciousness will allow individuals to embrace a more meaningful existence centered on connection, inner peace, and clarity.

Many have yet to realize that the true purpose of life is to become lighter, shedding the weight of worldly concerns and ego-driven desires.

The more we let go of these attachments, the closer we get to our original state of being.

If I like something, I give it away.

Something I've been doing for years, and I always feel lighter afterward.

Life is not about accumulation but about freeing ourselves from what holds us back, allowing us to move toward a higher spiritual understanding.

At the level of the High Council, our last stop in the material realms, we become almost transparent.

At the essence of this journey is the return to the Universal Consciousness, the light from which we all originated, freed from all materialistic desires.

This light represents the ultimate truth and purity that we are meant to rediscover.

As we evolve, both individually and collectively, we align ourselves with this higher consciousness, stepping back into the essence of where we originated.

The saying "as above, so below" reflects the connection between the spiritual and physical realms.

What happens in the higher planes mirrors what occurs in our earthly existence.

By understanding this, we can begin to live in alignment with universal truths, recognizing that the path to enlightenment lies in both our inner and outer worlds.

This planet is simply a reflection of our inner selves.

To break free

In accordance with the creation energy teachings, you choose to embrace ignorance over the profound truths inherent in creation and its laws, driven by a desire for societal standing and personal gain.

Your actions reveal a deep-seated cowardice as you submit to societal norms and fear the strictures imposed by any form of religion.

This fear stems from your inability to muster the courage to explore your true selves, to cultivate your own rational thoughts and intellect, and to embrace the genuine truth that transcends the falsehoods of religious beliefs in deities or idols.

As Billy explained, human beings of Earth, your behavior is perplexing. Upon rejecting traditional religious beliefs and disavowing falsehoods, you inadvertently create a backlash.

This rejection often leads to adopting another form of deity or idol, perpetuating a cycle where you become ensnared by a new religious or sectarian belief system.

These systems grip you just as tightly as the ones you previously abandoned, preventing you from discovering the genuine truth—the profound truth of creation and its immutable laws and recommendations.

The journey you embark upon from one religious belief to another does not bring you closer to understanding the ultimate truth.

Instead, it perpetuates a cycle of spiritual seeking devoid of genuine enlightenment.

True liberation lies in summoning the courage to question societal norms, explore your own intellect and reason, and seek the authentic truth that resides in the creation and its inherent laws and recommendations.

To break free from this cycle, you must overcome cowardice and fear and earnestly pursue a path that leads to genuine understanding and enlightenment.

Nurture the courage to confront your beliefs, cultivate your rational faculties, and discover the profound truth that transcends the transient allure of religious dogma and false idols.

Shaping my own path

I refrain from prayer because I have a clear understanding of my desires and aspirations.

Instead of seeking guidance or assistance through prayer, I rely on my own introspection and determination to achieve what I want in life.

This approach is grounded in a deep confidence in my own ability to direct my path.

My self-assurance empowers me to move forward with confidence and clarity.

By trusting in my own abilities and decisions, I am able to pursue my goals with a focused and determined mindset.

This personal conviction helps me manifest my aspirations effectively.

Navigating my journey without prayer means that I take full responsibility for my actions and their outcomes.

I have realized that through introspection and self-discipline, I can align my efforts with my goals and make informed choices that drive me toward success.

This new understanding, through the teachings of self-reliance, allows me to maintain a strong sense of purpose and direction.

By depending on my own strengths and insights, I am able to stay true to my aspirations and confidently shape my own path.

Resonance

Billy Meier, the Prophet of the New Time, brings you the pure truth, as clear and unadulterated as the sunlight that illuminates and warms you.

This truth serves as a beacon, guiding you toward liberation from all forms of darkness, evil, injustice, and irresponsibility.

Realizing the truth illuminates your path, fostering inner clarity and resilience against negativity and wrongdoing.

The purity of truth radiates like the sun, offering warmth and enlightenment to your soul.

It empowers you to discern right from wrong and to uphold fairness and righteousness in all aspects of life.

By internalizing this truth, you cultivate a moral compass that guides your actions toward harmony and justice.

As stated in the teachings, true prophets deliver messages that resonate with the essence of universal truth.

Their teachings inspire reflection and introspection, urging individuals to align their lives with principles that uphold dignity, compassion, and integrity.

Accepting their wisdom enables you to transcend personal limitations and contribute positively to the well-being of humanity.

The truth liberates you from the shackles of ignorance and discord.

It encourages you to live authentically, grounded in values that promote peace, justice, and mutual respect.

By embodying these principles, you foster a world where truth and righteousness prevail, enriching your own life and the lives of those around you.

Stewardship

By following the laws and guidance of Creation, you insulate yourself from the detrimental effects of evil and calamity.

These principles serve as a protective shield, offering resilience against adversity and ensuring a path toward inner peace and stability.

These guidelines foster a sense of security, knowing that you are aligned with universal truths that promote harmony and well-being.

Conversely, neglecting these principles exposes you to vulnerabilities.

As the teachings show, by deviating from the ethical and natural order prescribed by Creation, you risk encountering malevolence and hardship.

This can lead to profound disturbances in your inner well-being, causing turmoil and distress.

The consequences of disregarding these guidelines may manifest in various forms of personal and societal challenges.

The laws of Creation are designed to uphold justice, compassion, and sustainable living.

They encourage responsible stewardship of resources and harmonious coexistence with the environment and others.

By adhering to these principles, individuals contribute to a more equitable and peaceful world, safeguarding not only their own well-being but also that of future generations.

Trusting the laws and guidance of Creation empowers individuals to navigate life's challenges with clarity and resilience.

It reinforces the importance of ethical conduct and mindful decision-making, fostering a sense of purpose and fulfillment.

By aligning actions with these timeless principles, individuals uphold their integrity and contribute positively to the collective welfare of humanity.

The might of the thought

As the teachings introduce, the Creational laws dictate that personal inequity, suffering, and affliction stem solely from one's own thoughts.

There are no external forces, aside from one's own negative inclinations, wishes, or desires, that can disrupt an individual's sense of self or psyche.

External circumstances alone cannot cloud one's "I"-consciousness or inner state; any such disturbance originates internally.

Achieving true virtue, success, and happiness is not possible without consistent and virtuous effort.

The development of these qualities depends on ongoing, deliberate cultivation rather than external factors.

Success and happiness require a sustained commitment to positive actions and thoughts.

The power of thought plays a crucial role in shaping one's reality. Whether consciously or unconsciously, what one thinks will eventually manifest.

This means that individuals have the ability to create their own experiences and reality through their thoughts.

The nature of one's thoughts directly influences what becomes reality.

As a result, each person is the master of their own thinking and thus the architect of their mortality, character, psyche, and overall personality. The conscious management of thoughts shapes one's self-awareness, personal growth, and entire existence.

The creative force and the art

Humans embody both the creative force and the art itself.

At the core of each individual lies an innate creative energy, a fundamental drive that shapes and molds our experiences and expressions.

This creative essence is a powerful, dynamic force that fuels our ability to generate and transform ideas.

In the context of our existence, this internal creative energy manifests itself in various forms, giving rise to the beauty and complexity of our lives.

Every person, through their thoughts, actions, and creations, becomes a living expression of this intrinsic artistry.

As individuals navigate their journeys, they continuously contribute to the art of their lives through their unique perspectives and experiences.

The manifestations of this creativity are reflected in the diverse and rich tapestry of human expression, capturing the essence of our shared humanity.

Each human being serves as both the creator and the creation, combining their inherent artistic energy with their lived experiences.

This duality highlights the profound connection between the creative force within and the outward expression of that creativity, underscoring the intrinsic beauty in every individual.

Full attention

As the teachings stated, action is a constant presence in human life.

Every thought, feeling, and emotion is continually active, just as all physiological and physical processes, as well as the activities of the hands and the entire body, remain in motion.

This ongoing activity underscores the pervasive nature of our deeds.

A student of spiritual teachings faces two primary paths of self-determined development.

The first path involves dedicating full attention and evolutionary focus to all deeds and actions, thereby engaging deeply with the process of growth.

Alternatively, the student may choose not to engage in this focused manner, allowing actions and processes to proceed without deliberate consideration.

This choice reflects a different approach to personal and spiritual development.

The way one chooses to direct attention to one's actions and processes significantly influences their path of growth.

Whether through attentive engagement or a more passive approach, the nature of one's involvement in their deeds shapes their overall development.

Critical thinking

In today's world, it seems that many people have lost the ability to think independently.

This phenomenon reflects a broader issue where individual critical thinking is increasingly compromised.

The prevalent reliance on external sources for direction and validation often undermines personal autonomy and intellectual engagement.

Our current global environment fosters an atmosphere where conformity and passive reception of information are common.

This widespread tendency not only stifles individual thought but also diminishes the capacity for creative problem-solving and self-reflection.

The consequence is a society where personal agency and intellectual independence are at risk.

The path forward involves embracing the teachings of the Creation Energy.

These teachings offer valuable insights into cultivating personal awareness and self-reliance.

By engaging with these principles, individuals can begin to reclaim their capacity for independent thought and restore a sense of personal empowerment.

The sooner people start incorporating the wisdom of Creation Energy into their lives, the sooner they will be able to break free from the constraints of passive conformity.

This shift could lead to a more intellectually vibrant and self-determined society where people are better equipped to think critically and make informed decisions.

Believe

Starting your thinking with the word "believe" suggests that you are initiating your thought process from a place of doubt.

This inherent uncertainty means that the outcomes of your thoughts will be influenced by this doubt, potentially leading to conclusions that are not entirely true.

Consequently, this approach can hinder your ability to achieve clarity and understanding.

Furthermore, beginning with a belief can obstruct your connection to the subconscious mind, which houses the accumulated wisdom and knowledge from your past experiences and lives.

This detachment from the deeper aspects of your psyche can limit your access to valuable insights that could otherwise enrich your understanding.

In light of this, it is essential to move away from simply believing and instead focus on actively seeking knowledge.

By pursuing knowledge, you approach problems and questions with an open mind, free from the constraints of pre-existing doubts or assumptions.

This method encourages a more thorough and accurate exploration of ideas.

Replacing belief with a quest for knowledge allows for a more direct and meaningful engagement with your subconscious.

This shift can lead to a deeper comprehension of yourself and the world around you, tapping into the full spectrum of insights available to you.

Fulfilling lives

Truly, within the laws and recommendations of Creation exist profound treasures and invaluable guidelines for navigating life.

The teachings show that these principles are rooted in the natural order and wisdom inherent in the universe, offering a pathway to profound understanding and achievement.

Adhering to these principles with diligence and commitment ensures not only success but also fulfillment in all aspects of life.

They provide a framework for ethical conduct, sustainable practices, and harmonious relationships with both nature and fellow human beings.

These guidelines help individuals align themselves with universal truths that promote personal growth and societal well-being.

The treasures within these principles encompass a holistic approach to life, encompassing physical, mental, and spiritual well-being.

They emphasize the importance of balance, resilience, and compassion in navigating challenges and pursuing aspirations.

Each guideline serves as a beacon, guiding individuals toward a life rich in meaning and purpose.

Welcoming the laws and recommendations of Creation fosters a deeper connection to the world around us and encourages a harmonious existence.

It empowers individuals to lead fulfilling lives while contributing positively to the collective advancement of humanity.

By honoring these timeless principles, one embraces a journey of continuous learning and evolution guided by the profound wisdom embedded in the fabric of Creation.

Sustainable world

Hence, it is imperative to endeavor to be responsible and conscientious individuals, upholding the laws and guidance of Creation with fairness and integrity.

This commitment not only promotes personal growth but also contributes to the well-being and prosperity of both oneself and the community at large.

Undoubtedly, the teachings tell us living in accordance with the principles of Creation involves respecting the inherent order and harmony of the natural world.

It requires making decisions that prioritize ethical considerations and the long-term sustainability of resources.

By aligning actions with these fundamental laws, individuals foster a harmonious coexistence with nature and each other.

Fairness and integrity serve as cornerstones in the application of these principles.

They ensure that decisions are made impartially and ethically, considering the diverse needs and perspectives within society.

Upholding these values promotes trust and collaboration, which are essential for achieving collective goals and addressing societal challenges effectively.

Truly, grasping responsibility and conscientiousness cultivates a sense of purpose and fulfillment.

It empowers individuals to contribute positively to their surroundings, fostering a supportive environment where everyone can thrive.

By embodying these qualities, individuals not only enhance their own lives but also contribute to creating a more equitable and sustainable world for future generations.

Cultivating an open mind

Many individuals find it challenging to grasp the ultimate truth, and therefore, they require guidance to discern it.

Although there are various paths that can lead towards this truth, the truth itself remains singular and universal for every human being.

Understanding the truth often involves unraveling complexities and overcoming personal biases and misconceptions.

It requires a willingness to explore different perspectives and embrace uncertainty as part of the journey toward enlightenment.

As mentioned in the teachings, true wisdom emerges from a deeper comprehension of reality rooted in objective observations and introspective insights.

While diverse cultural and philosophical traditions offer distinct approaches to truth-seeking, they ultimately converge on fundamental principles that transcend individual beliefs.

These principles serve as guiding lights, illuminating the essence of existence and the interconnectedness of all beings.

By cultivating an open mind and a spirit of inquiry, individuals can embark on a transformative quest for truth.

This journey not only enriches personal growth but also fosters empathy and understanding toward others who may navigate their own paths toward discovering the profound truths that unite humanity.

Letting go of resentment and negativity

Allowing love, peace, freedom, and harmony to imbue your essence brings you a sense of security and tranquility.

These virtues serve as shields, offering comfort and reassurance in challenging times.

By welcoming them wholeheartedly, you create an inner sanctuary that nurtures positivity and resilience.

Letting go of resentment and negativity is essential for personal growth and well-being.

These emotions can weigh heavily on the spirit, hindering inner peace and clarity.

By releasing them, you open yourself to greater emotional freedom and a deeper connection with yourself and others.

Love, as a guiding force, encourages empathy and compassion towards oneself and others.

It fosters forgiveness and understanding, paving the way for healing and reconciliation.

Peace emerges when the mind and heart are at ease, free from turmoil and discord.

As confirmed in the teachings, harmony is achieved through balance and alignment within oneself and with the world around us.

It involves embracing diversity and fostering unity, promoting cooperation and mutual respect.

By cultivating these qualities, you contribute to a harmonious existence where love, peace, freedom, and harmony prevail.

Thanking God

Thanking God for another day of life carries an implicit belief that death has spared you while taking others, suggesting that you are favored more.

This viewpoint reflects a self-centered attitude that can lead to the notion of enjoying a heavenly afterlife while knowing that others are suffering in eternal torment.

Such thinking is fundamentally selfish and overlooks the suffering of loved ones.

This selfish mindset contributes to the idea that personal salvation is more important than the well-being of others, creating a paradox where one can seek heaven while acknowledging the pain of others.

This approach reveals a significant flaw in valuing one's own salvation over the collective suffering of humanity.

Many people on Earth have yet to grasp that a meaningful life involves living for the benefit of others.

True fulfillment comes from focusing on the well-being and support of those around us rather than seeking individual rewards or salvation.

Recognizing that life should be about serving and supporting one another rather than pursuing personal gain can lead to a more compassionate and interconnected existence.

By adopting this perspective, we can foster a deeper sense of empathy and shared humanity.

Avoiding fatigue

In line with the teachings, It is essential to consistently nurture love, integrity, and compassion in our relationships with others, ensuring these virtues remain steadfast and unwavering.

By doing so, we create a foundation of trust and mutual respect that enriches our interactions and strengthens our communities.

Love, as a guiding principle, encourages empathy and kindness towards others.

It fosters deep connections and promotes a sense of unity and belonging. Integrity ensures that our actions align with our values and principles, building credibility and trustworthiness in our relationships.

Compassion is crucial in understanding and alleviating the suffering of others.

It prompts us to offer support and comfort, fostering a culture of care and empathy within our social circles.

These virtues consistently contribute to a harmonious environment where everyone feels valued and respected.

Avoiding fatigue or uncertainty in practicing these virtues requires dedication and mindfulness.

It entails persevering through challenges and remaining steadfast in our commitment to love, integrity, and compassion, even during difficult times.

By prioritizing these qualities, we cultivate meaningful connections and create a positive impact on the lives of those around us.

Universal truth

Do not be afraid of the true prophets, for they come bearing good news.

Their teachings aim to foster a life where people can dwell together in goodness, love, harmony, and freedom.

By following the laws and guidance of Creation, their messages offer a pathway to a harmonious existence where each individual's well-being is respected and nurtured.

In sync with the creation energy teachings, the true prophets advocate for a way of life rooted in moral integrity and respect for natural laws.

Their teachings encourage unity and mutual understanding among people, promoting a society where compassion and justice prevail.

They envision a world where adherence to these principles leads to genuine peace and freedom for all.

It is through adherence to the laws and recommendations of Creation that their promises of harmony and freedom are realized.

By aligning oneself with these universal truths, one not only benefits personally but also contributes to the collective welfare of humanity.

The prophets' guidance serves as a beacon of hope, inspiring individuals to embrace love and goodness in their interactions with others.

Therefore, see the teachings of the true prophets without fear. Their message encourages a life filled with goodness, love, harmony, and freedom, underpinned by a deep reverence for the laws of Creation.

This path promises a future where humanity thrives in unity and mutual respect, guided by principles that uphold the sanctity of life and the well-being of all.

Shared vision

The teachings say adhering to the laws and guidance of the all-mighty Creation offers individuals the opportunity to cultivate profound virtues such as genuine love, freedom, peace, and harmony within themselves.

These virtues are not only to be embraced on a personal level but also shared among all human beings, fostering collective well-being and prosperity globally.

Genuine love, rooted in empathy and compassion, enables individuals to build meaningful connections and foster a sense of unity within diverse communities.

It encourages acts of kindness, understanding, and support, creating environments where individuals feel valued and cared for.

Freedom upheld through adherence to moral principles and ethical conduct empowers individuals to make choices that honor personal integrity while respecting the rights and freedoms of others.

It promotes justice, fairness, and equality, ensuring that every individual can live with dignity and autonomy.

Peace and harmony, nurtured through dialogue, cooperation, and mutual respect, cultivate environments where conflicts are resolved peacefully and differences are celebrated.

These virtues foster stability, resilience, and collaborative progress, paving the way for sustainable development and global unity.

By allowing these virtues to guide their actions and interactions, individuals contribute to the creation of a world where love, peace, freedom, and harmony are upheld as universal values.

Their commitment inspires others to embrace these principles, fostering a culture of empathy, understanding, and solidarity that transcends cultural and geographical boundaries.

Together, they work towards a shared vision of a compassionate and harmonious world for all humanity.

Upon death

Upon death, the human being's spirit departs with nothing but the wisdom and knowledge accumulated during their lifetime.

All material possessions remain within the material realm, separate from the spirit.

The essence of a human being transcends physical form.

It is fundamentally spiritual, embodying the Creation Energy.

Understanding this fundamental truth can profoundly shift one's perspective.

When people recognize that their true nature is spiritual rather than material, they are more likely to overcome materialistic desires.

This realization fosters a shift in focus from the pursuit of physical wealth to the nurturing of one's spiritual self.

As a result of this shift in focus, people will begin to prioritize their spiritual development.

This change in priorities leads to a more profound engagement with one's inner growth and evolution.

By valuing spiritual enrichment over material gain, people align more closely with their true essence.

Undoubtedly, grasping the nature of one's spiritual core can lead to a more fulfilling and purposeful life.

By emphasizing spiritual evolution over material accumulation, people can achieve a deeper sense of contentment and growth, reflecting the true nature of their being.

One's inner life

As the teachings prove, facial expressions, whether joyful or sullen, do not arise by chance; instead, they result from the influence of corresponding thoughts, which shape feelings and the state of the psyche. This, in turn, is reflected in one's facial appearance.

Often, disfiguring wrinkles on the face are a visible manifestation of one's inner life and thought patterns, distinct from those resulting from natural aging processes.

Many such wrinkles emerge from the misuse of thoughts, including foolish or negative thinking, self-inflicted suffering, and misguided expressions of pride.

These negative thought patterns can create deep lines and furrows that reveal an individual's inner turmoil.

The appearance of one's face can vary significantly with age based on their mental and emotional state.

For instance, some individuals may retain a youthful appearance into old age due to a positive and harmonious world of thoughts.

Conversely, others may exhibit pronounced, disharmonious features at a younger age, reflecting negative, self-pitying, or unsatisfied thought patterns.

In essence, the state of one's face and the presence of wrinkles are influenced by the quality of their thoughts.

A bright, happy, and harmonious psyche tends to maintain a youthful appearance, while negative and dissatisfied thoughts can lead to premature signs of aging and disharmony.

The prophets

According to the words of Billy, Due to the lack of earnest effort by many to deeply comprehend nature and the laws of Creation, true prophets have been dispatched.

These prophets' mission is to aid in understanding and interpreting the signs and evidence embedded within the natural world and the Creation's laws.

Their guidance is pivotal in illuminating these insights for the betterment of all humanity, enabling individuals to grasp and apply them effectively for personal and collective welfare.

The true prophets serve as intermediaries, bridging the gap between the complexities of nature and human understanding.

They elucidate the profound truths and principles inherent in the laws of Creation, offering clarity and guidance to those who seek knowledge and wisdom.

Through their teachings, individuals are empowered to discern and utilize these insights to navigate life's challenges and contribute positively to society.

The insights provided by the true prophets are essential for fostering a deeper connection with the natural world and aligning with the harmonious principles of Creation.

Their role extends beyond mere instruction; it encompasses fostering a spiritual and intellectual awakening among humanity.

By heeding their teachings, individuals can cultivate a profound reverence for nature and integrate these principles into their daily lives, promoting sustainability, compassion, and ethical conduct.

In essence, the presence of true prophets underscores the importance of seeking knowledge and wisdom about the laws of Creation.

Their guidance empowers individuals to embark on a journey of enlightenment and spiritual growth, enabling them to live in harmony with nature and uphold universal truths.

Through their efforts, humanity is encouraged to embrace a deeper understanding of existence and strive toward collective well-being and enlightenment.

Denying the ultimate truth

Consider that by pursuing desires that lack righteousness and by placing faith in divinities, praying to them irresponsibly, you burden yourselves heavily.

This burden stems from denying the ultimate truth and tethering yourselves to an imaginary god, elevating it as the creator of worlds and the universe.

Such actions lead to the homage paid in its name and the tragic consequences of warfare and punishment inflicted upon fellow human beings.

This misguided devotion to false deities perpetuates division, conflict, and suffering.

The teachings show that It distorts the fundamental principles of justice, compassion, and peace that should guide human interactions.

Instead of promoting unity and understanding, it fosters discord and enmity among individuals and communities.

To liberate yourselves from this burden, embrace the pursuit of righteousness and truth. Reject the worship of imaginary gods that sow seeds of division and violence.

Instead, cultivate a deeper understanding of the universal principles of love, compassion, and respect for all life.

By fostering a commitment to genuine spirituality and moral integrity, you contribute to a world where peace and harmony prevail.

Let us strive together to build a future where humanity is united in the pursuit of justice, equality, and mutual respect, transcending the false divides created by beliefs in imaginary gods.

Faces

In line with the principles of the creation energy teachings, faces reveal various aspects of an individual's inner life through their wrinkles and features, which can express feelings towards others or towards lower creatures.

Some faces show the imprint of strong and pure thoughts, while others display troubling signs of negative emotions, thoughts, and desires.

These expressions can be alarmingly evident, even to those who are not experts in physiognomy.

Often, the differences and signs on faces are so pronounced that even laypersons can discern whether a life has been lived positively or negatively.

The visible traits on a face can provide clear insights into the nature of one's life experiences and emotional states.

However, many people tend to observe the faces of others only superficially, missing the deeper meanings and life events that are recorded there.

As a result, they may not fully appreciate or understand the experiences and character revealed by these facial features.

Faces carry significant information about an individual's life and emotions, but this information is frequently overlooked.

To truly comprehend the depth of a person's experiences and character, one must look beyond surface appearances and recognize the subtle signs reflected in their expressions.

Mental fluidal powers

According to Billy, the human inclination towards seeking rational explanations for phenomena is evident when equipped with the requisite knowledge and cognitive tools to comprehend "amazing things" and other complex concepts.

However, the acknowledgment of mental fluidal powers remains absent both in parapsychological research and the realm of natural sciences.

Notably, there has been a glaring absence of investigative efforts from both natural scientists and parapsychologists in this regard.

This ignorance contributes significantly to widespread misunderstandings about human mental capabilities, fueling prejudices, delusions, and the proliferation of spiritualism and esoteric beliefs.

Consequently, diverse opinions, conflicts, confusions, and misinterpretations arise, accompanied by beliefs in ghosts, possession, exorcism, stigmatization, dowsing, and a profound inability to achieve true understanding.

Moreover, such misconceptions intensify existential anxieties among individuals, particularly regarding death, the devil, and ghosts, amplifying through religious doctrines that emphasize beliefs in evil spirits, demons, and ghostly apparitions.

The resultant conflicts frequently escalate into discord, quarrels, and animosity, often manifesting in religious or anti-religious rituals and practices such as exorcisms.

Tragically, these misunderstandings can lead to fatal consequences, such as the brutal mistreatment and killing of individuals suspected of being possessed by Satan or witches, reminiscent of historical inquisitions and persisting in contemporary sacrificial rituals aimed at purging evil spirits.

The urgency lies in the scientific community's delayed efforts to unravel the truth behind mental powers and fluidal energies, essential for dispelling pervasive delusions and superstitions.

Until clarity emerges on how these phenomena truly operate, the grip of delusional beliefs in "amazing things," spiritualism, exorcisms, and demonic possession will persist, perpetuating widespread fear and terror among vulnerable populations.

Such persistent delusions contribute to heightened psychological distress, pushing individuals with fragile mental states into psychiatric crises that jeopardize their mental health and rationality, potentially leading to irreversible psychological harm.

The imperative remains for scientists to diligently pursue the truth about mental fluidal powers, offering a pathway to dispel widespread superstitions and mitigate the profound social and psychological impacts of misconceptions surrounding human mental capabilities and supernatural phenomena.

The power of thoughts

One of the greatest lessons in the teachings is the fact that the power of thoughts can significantly diminish physical health and weaken the immune system, making the body more susceptible to illness.

When an individual anxiously battles an illness in their mind, it is often the case that such an illness eventually manifests physically.

The pervasive influence of negative, destructive, and harmful thoughts can thus lead to the emergence of health problems.

Beyond affecting personal health, these negative thoughts can have far-reaching effects on various aspects of life.

They can impact one's professional life, including work and business, as well as influence political activities and interactions with others.

This shows that the effects of negative thinking extend into numerous areas of one's external environment.

The destructive power of such thoughts is not limited to individual health but can also shape broader circumstances.

From influencing natural environments to affecting relationships, the consequences of negative thinking can be seen across many dimensions of life.

This highlights how deeply thoughts can affect not just the self but also external factors.

The influence of thoughts extends beyond personal well-being to impact various aspects of life, including work, commerce, politics, nature, and interpersonal relationships.

The pervasive nature of negative thoughts can thus create significant challenges and adverse outcomes in both personal and external spheres.

Anosognosic

What humans refer to as "God" is, in truth, Creation—the Universal Consciousness.

Creation is a pure, spiritual energy that exists far beyond the material world, making direct communication with human beings impossible.

It is not a personified entity but the source and essence of all life and existence, operating beyond the reach of human senses.

Even interacting with higher spiritual realms, such as the Arahat Athersata level, is incredibly energy-intensive, even for Billy.

Reaching these realms requires immense effort and is not easily accessible to those bound to the material world.

When people claim "God" has spoken to them, they are only deceiving themselves.

These claims are either born from wishful thinking or a misinterpretation of their own inner thoughts.

Creation does not send direct messages to individuals, and what people mistake for divine communication is merely a reflection of their own desires or wishes.

In reality, what is perceived as messages from God is simply the projection of their own thoughts and emotions.

Instead of receiving guidance from a higher source, they unknowingly attribute their inner wishes to a divine being.

This confusion between personal thoughts and spiritual truth is a common misunderstanding due to humanity's ignorance.

If you ever hear someone say, "God told me bla bla bla...", this person is anosognosic.

The Psyche

According to the creation energy teachings, the Psyche refers to the internal factor that influences one's mood, whether negative or positive, shaping the inner attitude.

This internal state, which is derived from the nature of one's thoughts and feelings, plays a crucial role in determining self-confidence.

A positive state can lead to feelings of exaltation, encouragement, joy, hope, and general emotional well-being.

Conversely, a negative state can give rise to despondency, joylessness, dejection, and hopelessness.

Essentially, the Psyche functions as a semi-material component within the material body of a living being, in this case, a human.

It organizes and manages thoughts and feelings within the material consciousness in a sequence that can be either negative or positive.

This results in either a negative or positive imbalance or a neutral, positive equilibrium.

Thus, humans can experience a state of being either negatively or positively out of balance or neutrally positively balanced.

When the Psyche is imbalanced in a positive or negative direction, it reflects a form of degeneration.

However, a neutrally positive balance indicates an equilibrium where negative and positive elements are equally present.

This state does not involve degeneration but rather achieves a state of symmetry and balanced harmony.

It is important to note that the Psyche should not be confused with the concept of the "Soul" as described by ancient philosophers like Plato, Aristotle, and Democritus or by the Stoics, Epicureans, and Greek mythology.

The Psyche, in this context, does not align with their traditional interpretations of the Soul.

Knowledge of truth

In congruence with the spiritual teachings, those who possess profound knowledge of truth shine like radiant stars in the vast expanse of the universe.

They embody the timeless principles and guiding truths that have shaped existence since its inception.

These individuals serve as beacons, reflecting the enduring laws and recommendations inherent in the fabric of Creation itself, offering clarity and direction to those who seek understanding.

The analogy of stars in the firmament underscores the transcendent nature of those who hold deep insights into truth.

Like stars illuminating the night sky, their wisdom and understanding illuminate the paths of others, guiding them through the complexities of life with clarity and purpose.

Their presence inspires awe and reverence, symbolizing the interconnectedness of all life and the universal truths that bind humanity together.

Furthermore, those with knowledge of truth serve as custodians of wisdom, preserving and transmitting ancient teachings and profound insights across generations.

They embody a deep connection to the essence of existence, drawing upon timeless principles to navigate challenges and promote harmony within themselves and their communities.

Their teachings resonate across cultures and epochs, offering enduring guidance in times of uncertainty and transformation.

In essence, individuals who possess knowledge of truth occupy a special role in the tapestry of human experience.

They bridge the gap between the mundane and the sublime, embodying the eternal truths that transcend temporal boundaries.

Through their insights and teachings, they contribute to the collective evolution of consciousness, fostering a deeper understanding of our place in the universe and our interconnectedness with all living beings.

Thoroughness

Thoroughness can be practiced in everyday tasks such as tidying up, washing dishes, or polishing a mirror through a conscious and artful approach.

In accordance with the teachings, It involves applying full concentration and attention to the task at hand, reflecting a deep respect for the reality of truth.

This purposeful action embodies the essence of thoroughness, honoring the present moment with meticulous care.

Thoroughness represents the foundational power behind every creation, from the absolute primordial origins to the impactful manifestations of relatively perfect forms.

It is akin to how a mighty tree grows from a small seed, illustrating the gradual yet powerful development that thoroughness facilitates.

In practice, thoroughness is closely linked with patience and a love for truth, serving as a driving force in the process of evolution.

By combining these qualities, one can effectively contribute to meaningful progress and improvement in various aspects of life.

Thoroughness, when paired with patience and dedication to truth, fosters significant growth and development.

It ensures that every action, no matter how small, contributes to the larger, evolving tapestry of creation.

Without worries

It is uncommon for people on Earth to live without worries clouding their minds.

These concerns disturb their inner peace, whether it's replaying past conversations and regretting unspoken feelings or fretting about immediate needs like rent, food, or their next fix.

Some even juggle the burden of lies, trying to remember past deceptions to maintain their façades.

The human mind is constantly bombarded by an array of problems.

When one tries to resolve these issues without achieving a state of calm, the confusion only intensifies.

Without inner peace, clarity of thought is hard to maintain, and this makes problems feel even more overwhelming as the mind becomes tangled in stress and disorder.

Yet, when inner peace is achieved, solutions to problems present themselves effortlessly.

In this state of mental stillness, answers arrive with ease, as if they had been waiting all along.

The mind, no longer cluttered by anxious thoughts, can focus on finding resolutions and making sound decisions.

True power lies within inner peace.

It is the key to unlocking clear thought, emotional stability, and the ability to face life's challenges with resilience.

In this calm space, people discover not only the solutions to their problems but also the strength to move forward with confidence.

Transformation

Through continuous study of the teachings, one can eventually witness the emergence of their true self, a process that unveils their most authentic nature.

This awakening allows individuals to shed the layers of external influence and self-doubt that once concealed their identity.

In reaching this state, they experience a transformation that aligns them more deeply with their inner purpose and truth.

The emergence of the true self brings a profound sense of freedom, liberating individuals from external pressures and the constraints of societal expectations.

With this freedom, they gain the strength to live in a way that genuinely reflects their desires and values, no longer feeling the need to conform or please others.

Their lives become a personal expression of choice, unaffected by outside influence.

As they continue to walk this path, they evolve into independent thinkers, unafraid to present themselves as they truly are.

This transformation leads to a heightened sense of integrity, where they can openly embody their truth without fear or compromise.

Living authentically becomes their natural state, enabling them to connect more deeply with themselves and others.

In this newfound authenticity, doubt and belief lose their grip, becoming relics of a former life governed by uncertainty and reliance on external validation.

Free from these limitations, individuals live with a quiet confidence grounded in self-awareness and understanding.

They transcend the need for belief, for their existence now rests on a foundation of inner clarity and assurance.

Develop patience

Human beings often speak about patience, yet it is a quality that can be consciously practiced every day.

Following the teachings, patience is a profound value of consciousness that can be cultivated through interactions with people, animals, plants, and any other material activity.

It involves recognizing and appreciating the true nature of time and finding freedom and space in each moment.

Learning patience requires acknowledging and navigating the irrational impulses and misunderstandings that disrupt our understanding of reality and the natural pace of evolution.

These misplaced impulses hinder the open creativity and effectiveness of our consciousness in the present.

To develop patience, one must confront and overcome these unreal and counterproductive impulses.

By doing so, individuals can align more closely with the ongoing processes of evolution and enhance their ability to respond effectively to the world around them.

Practicing patience means embracing and working with the natural rhythm of time and development.

This conscious effort allows for greater creativity and effectiveness in all aspects of life.

Fortitude

Indeed, attaining goodness and true understanding requires harnessing superior power, which can only be achieved through courageous strength, relentless effort, and a steadfast commitment to learning.

The teachings tell us that this journey demands resilience in the face of challenges and a willingness to persevere despite difficulties.

Without embodying these virtues, reaching the ultimate goal of enlightenment and insight becomes unattainable.

Courageous strength serves as a cornerstone in the pursuit of excellence and truth.

It empowers individuals to confront obstacles head-on, overcoming fear and doubt to forge ahead on their path of personal and spiritual growth.

This inner resolve fuels determination and inspires others through example, fostering a community of support and encouragement in the quest for knowledge and enlightenment.

Effort and diligence are indispensable companions on the journey towards achieving goodness and understanding.

The dedication to continuous learning and self-improvement drives individuals to expand their horizons and deepen their insights.

It requires a willingness to invest time and energy into acquiring knowledge and honing skills, laying the groundwork for transformative personal development and meaningful contributions to society.

Furthermore, fortitude is essential in maintaining steadfastness amid adversity and setbacks.

It instills resilience in facing challenges and setbacks with grace and determination, ensuring that setbacks do not derail progress but instead serve as valuable lessons in the pursuit of truth.

By cultivating fortitude, individuals cultivate inner strength and resilience, enabling them to persevere on their journey toward realizing their fullest potential and making a positive impact in the world.

True confidence

True confidence is best developed from within rather than relying on external validation.

When confidence is based on your own self-perception and values, it is less susceptible to fluctuations caused by external factors.

Building this inner strength allows you to maintain a stable sense of self-worth, regardless of external circumstances.

Depending on compliments and external praise for your confidence can be unstable and risky.

Praise is temporary and can be easily undermined by criticism or negative feedback.

If your confidence is based on external validation, it is more likely to falter when faced with disapproval or adverse opinions.

To achieve lasting confidence, focus on understanding and accepting yourself.

This involves recognizing your own strengths and areas for growth without depending on others' opinions.

Self-awareness and inner acceptance provide a solid foundation that helps you handle both positive and negative feedback with resilience.

Indeed, true confidence should come from deep-seated self-knowledge rather than external approval. \

By nurturing this internal confidence, you ensure that it remains strong and consistent, enabling you to navigate life's ups and downs with a stable and enduring sense of self-assurance.

The effectiveness of thoughts

The effectiveness of thoughts profoundly impacts physical well-being, influencing both sickness and health in various ways.

Beyond merely affecting health, thoughts also shape other life circumstances, as most human experiences stem from the power of thought.

As the teachings clearly show, negative, destructive thoughts manifest similarly in feelings, psyche, and bodily health, and they affect one's morality, character, and overall consciousness.

Additionally, external material conditions are also influenced by the nature of one's thoughts.

For example, thoughts rooted in anxiety or fear can be as detrimental as a physical weapon.

These emotions can profoundly impact health and well-being, potentially leading to severe consequences over time.

Anxiety and fear, if left unresolved, can cause significant harm comparable to the damage inflicted by physical threats, though often more gradual.

Moreover, persistent anxiety or fear about specific issues can eventually bring about those very issues.

A person who continually fears illness, for instance, is more likely to experience health problems related to that fear.

This illustrates how the power of thought can manifest in tangible, adverse outcomes.

The influence of thoughts extends beyond mere mental states to significantly impact physical health and life circumstances.

Persistent negative thoughts can lead to real health issues and affect one's overall quality of life, demonstrating the profound power of mental and emotional states in shaping our realities.

Courageous strength

When individuals forsake submissiveness and instead embrace courageous strength as their guiding force, according to the teachings, they tap into a superior power that propels them towards unwavering goodness and triumph over adversity.

Courageous strength signifies not only physical bravery but also mental fortitude and moral resilience, empowering individuals to confront challenges with determination and integrity.

This shift in mindset allows one to transcend limitations and approach obstacles with a steadfast resolve, fostering personal growth and achievement.

Courageous strength serves as a catalyst for personal transformation and empowerment. It encourages individuals to assert themselves assertively, making decisions based on principles rather than fear or hesitation.

This proactive approach enables them to navigate life's complexities with confidence and clarity, embodying resilience in the face of setbacks and uncertainties.

By realizing this inner strength, individuals cultivate a mindset of perseverance and optimism, enabling them to persevere through difficulties and emerge stronger.

Moreover, adopting courageous strength promotes a sense of moral courage and ethical integrity. It encourages individuals to uphold principles of justice and fairness, even in the face of opposition or adversity.

This steadfast commitment to doing what is right fosters trust and respect within communities, inspiring others to emulate similar values and actions.

By demonstrating moral courage, individuals contribute to a more ethical and harmonious society where integrity and compassion prevail.

The choice to abandon submissiveness in favor of courageous strength signifies a commitment to personal empowerment and positive change.

It embodies a proactive stance towards life, where challenges are viewed as opportunities for growth and learning.

By cultivating courageous strength, individuals not only enhance their own resilience and character but also inspire others to embrace bravery and integrity in pursuit of their goals and aspirations.

Moderation

Lack of moderation and modesty can lead to a cascade of negative consequences, exacerbating tendencies towards excess, hatred, jealousy, and insatiable desires.

In sync with the teachings, when moderation falters, it paves the way for avarice and a host of other destructive cravings, fostering stinginess, arrogance, and an insatiable thirst for recognition and glory.

These unchecked inclinations disrupt inner peace and societal harmony, contributing to unrest, oppression, and discord.

Immoderation breeds discontent and fosters an environment ripe for conflict and violence.

Indeed, according to the teachings, the absence of moderation allows unchecked desires and ambitions to escalate into battles and acts of aggression.

This imbalance undermines freedom and cultivates a state of bondage, where individuals and communities find themselves entrapped by unchecked impulses and conflicts arising from unbridled passions.

Moreover, the absence of moderation not only affects personal conduct but also disrupts social cohesion and stability.

It creates rifts between individuals and groups, fueling animosities and perpetuating cycles of discord.

The pursuit of excessive desires and the neglect of moderation erode empathy and mutual respect, replacing them with competitiveness and confrontation.

In contrast, embracing moderation and modesty fosters equilibrium and fosters a balanced approach to life.

It encourages restraint and thoughtful consideration in decision-making, promoting harmony and cooperation among individuals and within communities.

By cultivating moderation, individuals uphold principles of fairness and respect, contributing to a more peaceful and cohesive society where conflicts are mitigated through understanding and mutual goodwill.

Upon death

In accordance with the creation energy teachings, in you resides a spirit, a minute fragment of Creation, making you inherently a part of the cosmic whole.

However, your physical body belongs to your world, and upon death, it will cease to exist without transference to any heaven of deities or paradises of gods and idols.

Only the essence of your spirit within you is subject to reincarnation, destined to eventually reunite with Creation and merge with its essence.

As an individual, you will cease to exist in your current form, no longer continuing as you are known.

This perspective acknowledges the duality of existence: the mortal body tied to this world and the eternal spirit bound to the cycles of reincarnation and cosmic unity.

Your physical form, transient and finite, contrasts with the eternal journey of your spirit, which seeks eventual reunion with the greater whole of Creation.

Upon death, the body dissolves, finding no place among the heavens or paradises of the myriad gods and divine entities worshipped by mortals.

Instead, the enduring essence of your spirit persists, destined to traverse the cycles of rebirth until achieving union with the cosmic formation.

The teachings continue while your individuality as a person ceases with death; the spiritual essence within you persists beyond mortal bounds.

This essence, a fragment of Creation itself, undergoes the process of reincarnation, driven by the innate desire to reunify with the fundamental essence of the universe.

Thus, the cessation of your physical existence marks not an end but a transition in the perpetual journey toward oneness with the cosmic whole.

Death

We should not view death with disdain but instead embrace it as a natural part of life.

Just as youth and old age are inevitable, death too is a necessary stage in our existence.

It is no different from the physical changes we experience throughout life, such as growing new teeth, sprouting a beard, or seeing our first gray hair.

These transformations are a natural part of our journey, and death follows that same pattern.

Life involves many physical transitions, including sex, pregnancy, and childbirth, each marking a new phase.

Death is no different from these milestones.

It is simply another form of change, a natural dissolution of the body that completes the cycle of our existence.

We undergo many phases and death is just one more transition that occurs in due course.

A thoughtful person should not approach death with indifference, impatience, or contempt.

Instead, it should be viewed as one of the many inevitable events that happen to us.

It's not a tragedy or something to be feared, but a part of life, like all the other stages we pass through.

This understanding brings peace and allows us to face it calmly.

In the same way, we anticipate the birth of a child, waiting for its emergence from the mother's womb.

We should await our own final moment with similar acceptance, recognizing that it is simply the time for our spirit to emerge from the body.

Death, like birth, is a transition to be met with calm and openness.

The cycle of ignorance

The teachings tell us throughout history, numerous clear signs and evidence affirming the truth and existence of Creation, along with its laws and guidance, have been presented to humanity by authentic proponents of truth.

These teachings have been available since ancient times, yet humanity has often chosen to exchange this profound gift for the falsehoods of belief in various deities and idols.

Consequently, this decision has led to self-inflicted punishment, a cycle that persists to this day.

The rejection of truth in favor of erroneous beliefs has resulted in prolonged ignorance and suffering for humanity.

According to the teachings, it will require a considerable span of time before the truth is fully perceived and comprehended.

During this period, individuals will continue to dwell in falsehood, unaware of their misguided state, which will perpetuate their engagement in wrongful deeds and the consequent burden of guilt.

The journey towards recognizing and embracing the truth is lengthy and arduous.

Humanity, in its misguided state, will endure significant suffering as a consequence of its ignorance and misdeeds.

Ramifications of rejecting the teachings of truth extend through time, as individuals remain unaware and consequently continue to perpetuate actions that bring harm and guilt upon themselves.

In ending, the ongoing prevalence of falsehoods and the rejection of truth have caused humanity to endure a prolonged period of suffering and wrongdoing.

Only through a gradual process of realization and understanding will individuals begin to alleviate themselves from this cycle of ignorance and its resultant consequences.

The cycle of competition

Each life holds its own unique qualities, contributing to the overall beauty of existence.

Yet, humans on Earth consistently seek to surpass their neighbors, caught in a cycle of competition.

No matter how much wealth or success is gained, there is always someone with more, leading to an endless pursuit that never brings true satisfaction.

This search for superiority only perpetuates discontent as individuals chase something that can never truly fulfill them.

The wisdom of "use what you need and leave the rest" holds great significance.

What we leave behind is ultimately what we inherit, reminding us that balance and harmony are essential for lasting peace.

The ancestors we believe are watching over us are actually reflections of ourselves - we are our ancestors, continuing the cycle of existence.

This deeper understanding reveals that we are the guardians of our own destiny, and peace begins within each of us.

A new way of thinking is being introduced to humanity by Nokodemion, the Herald of this universe, through Billy Meier, the proclaimer of truth for the New Age.

These teachings offer Earth humans the guidance needed to finally achieve the peace that has long been sought.

By moving away from the endless pursuit of material gain and embracing wisdom and inner growth, humanity can find the elusive peace that has escaped us for so long.

This new thought process provides the key to ending the cycle of competition and discontent.

Through the wisdom of Billy Meier and the teachings, Earth humans have the opportunity to embrace a future built on cooperation, understanding, and peace.

Mental equilibrium

Suffering in human beings often originates from the powerful influence of their thoughts.

This suffering arises as a result of mental disharmony, where discord within one's mind manifests through their thoughts and feelings.

When an individual's thoughts are conflicted or unbalanced, they contribute to emotional turmoil and distress.

The teachings indicate this internal discord creates a fertile ground for suffering to take root, affecting both their mental and emotional well-being.

Thus, the nature of one's suffering can be traced back to the state of their thoughts and feelings.

Mental disharmony inevitably shapes and exacerbates the experience of suffering, highlighting the intricate connection between mental processes and emotional states.

By fostering mental equilibrium and resolving internal conflicts, individuals can mitigate the adverse effects of suffering and enhance their overall sense of well-being.

Addressing and harmonizing one's thoughts can, therefore, play a critical role in alleviating suffering.

The collective experience

The teachings indicate that our existence in this world is purposefully structured to facilitate your learning and fulfillment of life's meaning.

This journey unfolds through the evolution of knowledge and wisdom, as well as the pursuit of love, peace, freedom, and harmony, which collectively embody truth and reality.

These principles are intended not just for you individually but for all beings around you.

The essence of your life's journey is intricately tied to the acquisition of knowledge and the cultivation of wisdom.

As you progress, you are meant to deepen your understanding of love, peace, freedom, and harmony, integrating these virtues into your daily existence.

By embracing these ideals, you contribute to the realization of truth and the manifestation of reality within your own life and within the broader community of humanity.

Love, as a guiding principle, encourages empathy, compassion, and unity among individuals.

Peace fosters tranquility and the resolution of conflicts, promoting stability and well-being.

Freedom empowers individuals to pursue their aspirations and express their true selves without inhibition.

Harmony nurtures cooperation and mutual respect, fostering a cohesive and supportive social fabric.

At the end, the fulfillment of these ideals transforms them from mere concepts into tangible realities that shape your life's purpose.

As you navigate your journey, striving to embody these principles, you not only enrich your own existence but also contribute positively to the collective experience of humanity, forging a path towards greater understanding, unity, and fulfillment for all.

Human beings

Human beings must view themselves not just from a biological and mental perspective but also from a psychic and spiritual one.

These deeper dimensions offer a more complete understanding of who we are and what we are capable of becoming.

Hidden within the subconscious mind are the lessons, knowledge, and experiences accumulated over countless lifetimes.

Though these remain out of everyday awareness, they are always present, shaping our actions and choices in subtle ways.

Deep inside, there is a longing to tap into this well of wisdom and understanding.

It is an inner desire to rediscover and reconnect with the abilities, experiences, and knowledge we have gained through time.

To access this inner potential, individuals must first acknowledge and accept its existence.

By embracing this truth, they can unlock the dormant power within and make use of the vast resources that lie hidden beneath the surface.

Human consciousness

As the Herald stated, there is much that remains beyond our current understanding due to the limitations of our abilities and senses.

Not only are there many connections that span beyond the confines of space and time, which we must explore through heightened consciousness, but there is also the matter of the spirit-form.

As outlined by the teachings, this minute aspect of Creation animates human consciousness, influencing the mental and consciousness blocks as well as the physical body.

However, this spirit-form cannot be perceived through material senses like sight, hearing, touch, smell, or taste.

Instead, it is recognized only through a finer spiritual perception that emerges from the spirit realm and is processed through the subconscious into the material psyche and consciousness.

It is essential to acknowledge that phenomena extending beyond space and time are not detectable by our human senses.

These phenomena exist on more subtle, fluid levels and can only be perceived through specific means, such as the spiritual Gemüt, which is capable of fine-spiritual perception.

Unfortunately, humanity on Earth has yet to uncover logical, intellectual evidence for these finer perceptions.

The prevailing religious, ideological, and philosophical beliefs often trap individuals in irrational teachings that stray far from the truths of spiritual life.

The true spiritual life is rooted in Creation, its inherent love, laws, and recommendations, all of which exist beyond the material dimensions of space and time.

To truly grasp and understand these concepts, a deeper exploration and understanding beyond earthly scales is necessary. This involves expanding your awareness and consciousness to perceive the finer aspects of existence.

To recognize and understand these truths, it is crucial to move beyond the limitations of current beliefs and perceptions.

This requires an open-minded approach to exploring the spiritual realm and acknowledging that the essence of Creation and its laws are far beyond the immediate and tangible aspects of human experience.

Only through such an expansion of understanding can one truly appreciate the deeper realities of existence.

The wise

In the teachings, it's mentioned that strong, calm, knowledgeable, and wise individuals who embody peace, joy, love, and open-mindedness are highly valued and respected by the majority of humanity.

Such people, with their practical lived experiences, serve not only as examples but also as sources of inspiration for others to adopt similar qualities.

They are esteemed because they align with fundamental principles and recommendations that guide human behavior.

For those in search of life's deeper truths, these individuals are akin to vibrant trees in a parched and barren land.

They provide vital shade and nourishment, symbolizing hope and vitality.

Their presence offers respite and guidance to those who are seeking clarity and understanding amidst the challenges and confusion of life.

Their influence extends beyond mere inspiration; they serve as protectors against ignorance and the metaphorical 'living dead.'

By embodying the essence of wisdom and practical experience, they safeguard others from falling into a state of disillusionment or spiritual stagnation.

These remarkable individuals play a crucial role in fostering a more enlightened and compassionate society.

Their impact is profound, as they help others navigate their paths with greater insight and integrity, contributing to a more meaningful and connected human experience.

The current peace symbol

The symbol commonly known as the "death rune," derived from the Celtic Futhark runes or the inverted Algiz rune, represents a significant negative influence.

It evokes destructive energies associated with unpeace, hatred, revenge, vice, addictions, and bondage.

For many, this symbol brings to mind memories of the Nazi era, death, and devastation, and it perpetuates ambitions related to war, terror, and global discord.

As the teachings showed, it is crucial to eliminate the "death rune" from global usage and instead promote the correct and ancient peace symbol.

The true peace symbol embodies peace, freedom, harmony, and wisdom, offering a constructive and soothing impact.

It fosters positive energies and supports the development of peaceful and harmonious waves.

We call upon all individuals committed to peace and progress to actively promote the authentic peace symbol.

It is also essential to clarify the dangers and destructive potential of the "death rune," which continues to evoke harmful memories and behaviors linked to historical atrocities.

Replacing the "death rune" with the true peace symbol is a vital step toward healing and progress.

By disseminating the genuine symbol of peace and addressing the destructive legacy of the "death rune," we can help create a more harmonious world and mitigate the ongoing negative influences stemming from past conflicts.

The pursuit of pleasure

The dynamic energies and inherent powers within human beings propel them to seek esteem, honor, and various pleasures that enrich their existence.

According to Billy, These desires stem from fundamental aspects of human nature: the innate drive for self-preservation, the aspiration for admiration, and the pursuit of enjoyment.

These drives collectively shape human motivations and behaviors, influencing their aspirations and pursuits throughout life.

The drive for self-preservation manifests as a fundamental instinct to sustain life and ensure survival.

It prompts individuals to seek security, comfort, and fulfillment of basic needs, laying the groundwork for more complex desires and ambitions.

This foundational drive underpins human actions aimed at ensuring personal well-being and continuity in the face of challenges and uncertainties.

Similarly, the desire for admiration motivates individuals to seek recognition, respect, and validation from others.

It fuels aspirations for achievement and excellence, compelling individuals to strive for success and acclaim in various facets of life.

This drive plays a pivotal role in shaping social interactions, personal accomplishments, and contributions to society, influencing the pursuit of goals that enhance personal worth and reputation.

Furthermore, the pursuit of pleasure drives human beings to seek enjoyable experiences and gratifying sensations that enhance the quality of life.

Whether through sensory pleasures, intellectual pursuits, or emotional fulfillment, this drive prompts individuals to seek moments of happiness, satisfaction, and contentment.

It encompasses a wide spectrum of experiences that contribute to overall well-being and contribute to the richness of human existence.

In essence, these inherent drives—self-preservation, admiration, and pleasure—constitute fundamental motivations that propel human beings to pursue esteem, honor, and diverse pleasures.

They reflect core aspects of human nature, influencing personal aspirations, societal interactions, and the quest for fulfillment and meaning in life.

Understanding and navigating these drives contribute to a deeper appreciation of human behavior and the complex dynamics that shape individual experiences and collective aspirations.

Alignment with universal laws

Amidst the myriad terms and concepts used for self-reflection, the essence remains: to deeply understand oneself—thoughts, feelings, passions, habits, capabilities, and potentials.

Following the teachings, this introspective journey is crucial for delving into the core of existence, utilizing all perceptions, cognitions, and experiences to uncover the fundamental truths.

It involves integrating knowledge, practical wisdom gained from lived experiences, and the resulting insights to align with the universal truths inherent in Creation and its guiding principles.

The quest for self-knowledge encompasses a comprehensive exploration of one's inner landscape.

By examining thoughts and emotions, acknowledging strengths and weaknesses, and recognizing habitual patterns, individuals embark on a path toward deeper self-awareness.

This process not only enhances personal growth but also lays the foundation for a more meaningful connection with the broader truths that govern existence.

Furthermore, the journey toward truth involves synthesizing practical experiences with wisdom gained through introspection and learning.

It entails applying this accumulated wisdom to navigate life's complexities with integrity and clarity.

By aligning actions with the laws and recommendations of Creation, individuals facilitate their own evolution of consciousness, contributing to a broader harmony and understanding within the universe.

Ultimately, the pursuit of truth and alignment with universal laws leads to profound personal and spiritual growth.

It fosters a holistic approach to life, where self-discovery and ethical awareness converge to enrich both individual well-being and collective societal progress.

Embracing this journey with dedication and mindfulness enables individuals to contribute meaningfully to the interconnected tapestry of existence, guided by the pursuit of truth and the principles of Creation.

Physical fitness

It is futile to focus solely on physical fitness without making any effort toward evolving your consciousness.

Engaging in regular fitness training, taking walks, and participating in various activities to maintain bodily health are valuable practices.

However, these efforts become ineffective if they are not accompanied by a parallel growth in consciousness.

Indeed, the teachings demonstrate that physical fitness alone cannot prevent the inevitable aging and decay of the body.

The body is subject to natural processes of aging, which continue regardless of how well you take care of it.

Without a corresponding evolution of consciousness, the body's physical state remains disconnected from deeper personal development.

To truly benefit from physical exercises and maintain overall well-being, it is essential that these efforts align with the progression of your consciousness.

Both the physical and mental aspects of health must be nurtured in tandem to achieve a balanced state of being.

Ignoring the development of consciousness while focusing solely on the body will not yield lasting results.

For a holistic approach to health, it is crucial to integrate the growth of consciousness with physical fitness.

This unified approach ensures that as your body ages and changes, your consciousness continues to evolve, fostering a more complete and harmonious state of well-being.

The pursuit of righteousness

To attain equitableness and moderation, it is essential to practice moderation in all aspects of life and not veer excessively from the path of good human nature.

In accordance with the teachings, this entails navigating life's highs and lows with righteousness and responsibility, always learning and remaining connected to the fundamental truths encapsulated in the laws and guidance of universal consciousness or Creation.

Moderation serves as a cornerstone for cultivating equitableness and modesty, fostering a balanced approach to interactions and decisions.

It involves maintaining a harmonious equilibrium in thoughts, actions, and desires, avoiding extremes that may lead to imbalance or ethical lapses.

By embracing moderation, individuals nurture a stable foundation for ethical behavior and fair dealings with others, grounded in principles that transcend personal gain.

Equally important is the pursuit of righteousness and conscientiousness throughout life's journey.

This involves aligning one's actions with moral principles and ethical standards, striving to uphold fairness and responsibility in all circumstances.

By adhering to these principles, individuals uphold their commitment to integrity and contribute positively to the social fabric, promoting justice and equity in their interactions and communities.

Furthermore, staying attuned to the truths and insights derived from universal consciousness or Creation enhances one's understanding of ethical conduct and interconnectedness with the world.

This spiritual and philosophical alignment fosters a deeper appreciation for the interconnectedness of all life and guides individuals toward actions that promote harmony and mutual respect.

By integrating these principles into daily life, individuals not only cultivate personal growth but also contribute to a more just and compassionate society where equitableness, moderation, and ethical responsibility thrive.

Provoke

Based on the teachings, to be heard, you often need to provoke a reaction, which can involve causing offense.

This is because people tend to notice and engage with information more deeply when it challenges or irritates them.

Repetition is also crucial; if you want to ensure that your message is noticed, you may need to present the same facts multiple times.

This repetition, whether it causes irritation or discomfort, forces people to confront the information.

The goal is to make people think, regardless of whether their reaction is peaceful or angry.

The essential aspect is the impact on their awareness and response.

When people feel provoked or attacked, they are more likely to engage with the ideas being presented, leading to reflection and reaction.

Soft and flattering language is often ineffective for conveying truth.

If your intention is to make a meaningful impact, gentle words are unlikely to achieve this.

The reality is that truth frequently requires a more direct and sometimes uncomfortable approach to cut through complacency and spark genuine thought.

The effectiveness of communication lies in its ability to provoke thought and reaction, even if it involves offending or challenging the listener.

Only through such methods can you ensure that your message is not ignored and that it prompts the desired level of consideration and engagement.

Fairness

Human beings are urged to uphold fairness consistently in their interactions, whether with friends or adversaries.

Based on the creation energy teachings, this commitment to equitableness ensures readiness to reciprocate justly in every situation, rewarding fairness with fairness itself.

It underscores the importance of maintaining integrity in negotiations by seeking and offering honest terms, thereby fostering trust and mutual benefit.

Equally crucial is the responsibility to avoid any form of deception or exploitation, preserving the ethical foundation of all dealings.

Practicing fairness not only strengthens interpersonal relationships but also promotes a more equitable society.

By treating others justly, individuals contribute to a culture where respect and honesty prevail, enhancing cooperation and understanding.

This principle extends beyond personal interactions to encompass broader societal frameworks, guiding ethical behavior in all spheres of life.

It serves as a cornerstone for building trust and fostering meaningful connections that endure through challenges and differences.

Moreover, fairness serves as a safeguard against exploitation and inequality, ensuring that all parties are treated with dignity and respect.

It encourages individuals to uphold principles of justice and equality, reinforcing the fabric of societal norms and expectations.

By prioritizing fairness, human beings uphold their moral duty to contribute positively to their communities, fostering environments where fairness and integrity thrive.

Eventually, the practice of equitableness reflects a commitment to ethical conduct and responsible citizenship, shaping a world where fairness is a guiding principle in all endeavors.

The unreal impulses

Human beings have the choice to use everyday life, as well as space and time, to practice and develop conscious values—or not.

According to the teachings, Consciousness-based values help to open the material consciousness to spiritual impulses, creating a pathway to connect with these creational forces.

This decision is ultimately up to each individual, determining whether they will engage with their daily life in a manner that is consciously valuable or merely materialistic.

Each person has the power to shape their experiences through their will.

They must choose what holds greater significance: whether to focus on a reality-oriented, clear consciousness or on transient material concerns.

The choice lies between recognizing true value or being captivated by fleeting illusions.

Individuals also decide whether to be guided by the unreal impulses of an untrained material consciousness or by the effective knowledge, wisdom, and logic of a well-trained, clear consciousness.

This choice involves consciously and concentratively working on one's consciousness every day.

The universe's system is open to human beings, allowing them to act on its causes to awaken and evolve specific consequences.

By making deliberate choices, individuals can influence their path and development, aligning their actions with the broader cosmic principles.

Compassion and altruism

Compassion, driven by a genuine love for fellow human beings and for life itself, manifests as a gentle influence on all thoughts and intentions directed towards oneself, animals, plants, and others.

It transcends mere moral or philosophical concepts, embodying a profound and tangible alignment with the forces of life and existence.

This alignment is a resonance with reality and its inherent truths, encompassing understanding, happiness, joy, and vitality.

According to Billy, compassion fosters a deep connection to the essence of life, resulting in a sense of fulfillment through the pursuit of justice.

In daily life, compassion leads human beings to channel their thoughts and feelings through the fundamental value of altruism.

Altruism, in this context, is characterized by modesty, a deep understanding of life, and a conscious dedication to observing and engaging with it.

Compassion and altruism together guide individuals toward a meaningful and harmonious existence.

As the teachings stated, by embracing these values, people cultivate a genuine connection with life, contributing to a more just and fulfilling world.

Equitableness

Following the teachings, it's important to distinguish between fairness and equitableness as they carry distinct meanings and implications. Equitableness is rooted in the steadfast adherence to what is morally right and just.

It requires a resolute commitment to upholding principles of righteousness in all actions and decisions, ensuring that fairness is consistently applied in every situation.

This entails a steadfast dedication to preserving and advocating for what is right while ensuring that each individual receives their due.

Equitableness is not merely about being impartial or neutral; rather, it embodies a proactive stance in safeguarding justice and ethical conduct.

It involves actively defending and promoting the rights and entitlements of every person, regardless of circumstances or biases.

This commitment demands a strong sense of moral responsibility and a willingness to uphold fairness as a guiding principle in interactions and decisions.

Central to equitableness is giving each individual what rightfully belongs to them.

This includes not only material possessions but also respect, dignity, and opportunities for growth and fulfillment.

By adhering to equitable practices, individuals contribute to a harmonious and just society where everyone is treated with integrity and compassion.

As a result, equitableness reflects a deep-seated commitment to ethical behavior and justice.

It requires individuals to actively pursue what is right and just, fostering an environment where fairness and integrity prevail.

By nurturing equitableness as a guiding principle, individuals contribute to a world where each person's rights and contributions are valued and respected, promoting collective well-being and societal progress.

Seeking reality

When embarking on a quest for understanding, consistent with the teachings, prioritize seeking reality through truth from beginning to end.

This approach ensures that every discovery and realization transcends initial expectations, enriching the searcher's journey with profound insights and wisdom.

By steadfastly aligning with truth, individuals open themselves to deeper understanding and fulfillment beyond mere surface-level findings.

Critical discernment plays a pivotal role in this pursuit, guiding individuals to distinguish between truth and falsehood.

It empowers them to reject deceit, illusion, negligence, bias, and any conduct contrary to fairness.

This discernment fosters clarity of thought and action, enabling individuals to navigate complexities with integrity and ethical resolve.

As the teachings show, connecting with truth requires a deliberate commitment to authenticity and sincerity.

It involves setting aside superficial or deceptive notions and embracing honesty in all aspects of inquiry and interaction.

This steadfast adherence to truth cultivates trust and credibility, both within oneself and in relationships with others, fostering harmonious and meaningful connections.

Embracing truth as a guiding principle empowers individuals to transcend personal biases and societal illusions.

It encourages a mindset of openness and receptivity to new perspectives, promoting continuous growth and enlightenment.

By valuing truth above all else, individuals forge a path toward genuine understanding and contribute positively to a world built on principles of integrity, fairness, and ethical conduct.

Cornerstone of decision-making

The key to making sound decisions and achieving success lies in the application of rationality and intellect, grounded in alignment with objective truth.

In harmony with the teachings, rational thought and keen discernment prove essential when individuals connect themselves to the inherent truths that demonstrate their potency across all circumstances and choices.

Without anchoring cognition and intellect in truth, their potential remains as fleeting and inconsequential as smoke dissipating in the air.

Rationality and intellect attain significance only when employed in pursuit of truth and righteousness.

They empower individuals to navigate complexities by accurately assessing situations and making informed choices.

Whether applied to thoughts, emotions, speech, or actions, these faculties derive their effectiveness from their alignment with truth and their ethical application.

Truth serves as the guiding principle that lends credibility and purpose to rational thought and intellectual discernment.

By adhering to truth, individuals ensure their decisions are rooted in integrity and moral clarity, fostering outcomes that are beneficial and just.

This alignment enables them to confront challenges with clarity and resolve, promoting personal growth and contributing positively to their communities.

At last, the integration of truth with rationality and intellect enables individuals to wield these faculties effectively in their pursuit of meaningful goals.

By valuing truth as the cornerstone of decision-making and action, individuals harness the full potential of their cognitive abilities to navigate life's complexities with wisdom and purpose.

Embracing life's challenges

Life continually presents human beings with fresh challenges, questions, and complexities to navigate.

In compliance with these teachings, each day unfolds with new tasks, difficulties, and mysteries that require understanding or exploration.

These experiences compel individuals to embark on unfamiliar paths, prompting them to make daily decisions and engage with life in constantly evolving ways.

The dynamic nature of life demands adaptability and resilience from individuals as they confront the unforeseen and the unknown.

From confronting personal dilemmas to unraveling enigmatic aspects of existence, human beings are constantly tasked with expanding their understanding and capabilities.

This perpetual process of growth and discovery shapes their journey and influences their perspectives.

Navigating life's challenges involves not only problem-solving but also continuous learning and self-discovery.

Each encounter with adversity or uncertainty offers opportunities for personal development and the acquisition of new insights.

By confronting these challenges head-on, individuals acquire the wisdom and experience needed to make informed decisions and face future uncertainties with confidence.

Grasping the ever-changing nature of existence requires an open mind and a willingness to engage actively with life's complexities.

It encourages individuals to approach each day with curiosity and determination, seeking to uncover truths, overcome obstacles, and evolve personally and intellectually.

By embracing life's challenges as opportunities for growth and exploration, individuals can forge a path of continual self-improvement and fulfillment.

Persecuting virtues

Indeed, individuals who are disconnected from virtues and actively oppose them are also undermining the principles inherent in the laws and recommendations of creation.

Persecuting virtues equates to rejecting the ethical foundations that guide human conduct toward fairness, justice, and moral integrity.

Following Billy's words, such actions not only discredit these principles but also reflect a disregard for the inherent dignity and rights of others.

Persecution of truth extends beyond mere disbelief or ignorance; it involves actively opposing and discrediting the pursuit of knowledge and wisdom.

Those who persecute truth undermine efforts to uphold fairness and integrity in society, perpetuating falsehoods and injustice.

This undermines the foundations of a harmonious and equitable social order.

Individuals who persecute truth and virtuous behavior often resort to slander and defamation against those who embody these principles.

By attacking individuals who possess knowledge and advocate for truth, they seek to undermine credibility and discredit moral authority.

This tactic aims to suppress dissent and discourage others from embracing ethical values and pursuing truth.

Conclusively, the persecution of virtues and truth reflects a broader pattern of intolerance and moral corruption.

It hinders societal progress towards a more just and compassionate world by promoting division and distrust.

Embracing virtues and advocating for truth is essential for fostering a society built on mutual respect, fairness, and the pursuit of the common good.

By valuing and upholding these principles, individuals contribute to the collective effort of promoting integrity and dignity for all.

Benevolence

As asserted by Billy, finding happiness and contentment comes from dedicating oneself to benevolence and compassion towards humanity.

Those who are connected to benevolence are not only capable of helping themselves in times of distress but also extend their support to others—whether they are neighbors, acquaintances, or strangers in need.

This includes aiding the poor, the needy, the sick, the unfortunate, and those who may have strayed from ethical paths.

Engaging in acts of benevolence involves not only providing material assistance but also offering emotional support and understanding to those facing difficulties.

It encompasses a spirit of empathy and solidarity that transcends individual circumstances, fostering a sense of community and shared humanity.

Supporting others in distress or need reflects a commitment to upholding values of compassion, justice, and mutual aid.

It acknowledges the interconnectedness of human experiences and the importance of collective well-being.

By extending kindness and assistance to others, individuals contribute to the creation of a supportive and inclusive society.

Indeed, happiness derived from benevolence stems from the fulfillment found in making a positive difference in the lives of others.

It affirms the value of human dignity and the power of empathy in fostering meaningful connections and promoting social harmony.

By engaging in benevolence as a guiding principle, individuals not only enhance their own well-being but also contribute to building a more compassionate and resilient community.

Harmonious existence

Happiness is found in the compassionate act of providing sustenance to those in need, offering relief to the hungry and thirsty.

Similarly, as told in the teachings, as human beings, there is a profound hunger and thirst for true love, knowledge, wisdom, fairness, peace, freedom, and harmony.

Fulfilling these spiritual and intellectual needs brings fulfillment and joy, achievable through a dedicated pursuit of truth and adherence to the laws and recommendations of creation.

The act of providing food and drink to the hungry and thirsty exemplifies empathy and generosity, essential qualities that foster a sense of community and mutual support.

This compassion extends beyond physical nourishment to encompass the emotional and spiritual fulfillment that comes from seeking and sharing truth, love, and wisdom.

Human beings are inherently driven by a quest for deeper understanding and fulfillment.

Pursuing truths about love, knowledge, fairness, peace, and freedom aligns individuals with higher principles that enrich personal growth and societal harmony.

By employing these values and adhering to creational laws, individuals contribute positively to their own well-being and that of others, fostering a harmonious existence.

Happiness and fulfillment are realized through a meaningful pursuit of truth and a commitment to ethical living.

By nourishing the mind and soul with knowledge, wisdom, and virtues such as fairness and harmony, individuals cultivate a sense of purpose and satisfaction.

This journey towards personal and collective enlightenment underscores the importance of aligning actions with principles that promote mutual respect, justice, and compassion in the pursuit of a more harmonious world.

Ethical living

As outlined in the teachings, solace is also reserved for those who suffer from the consequences of wrongdoing inflicted upon them by the actions of fellow human beings against the principles of universal truth and the laws of creation.

Such individuals experience profound sorrow and anguish due to the prevalence of heinous crimes, senseless violence, suppression of truth, wars, hatred, jealousy, enmity, vengeful tendencies, and other destructive behaviors that sow discord and suffering throughout the world.

The recognition of these injustices underscores the need for compassion and empathy towards those who endure the consequences of human misdeeds.

It acknowledges the profound impact of immoral actions on individuals and communities, highlighting the urgency of addressing root causes and promoting ethical conduct.

Crimes against truth and humanity, including acts of violence and oppression, reflect a departure from the principles of justice and harmony inherent in the laws of creation.

They disrupt societal cohesion and undermine efforts to foster peace, cooperation, and mutual respect among people.

In facing these challenges, there is a collective responsibility to uphold moral integrity and strive for reconciliation and healing.

Amidst the calamities wrought by human actions, there remains hope for redemption and renewal.

By acknowledging wrongdoing and actively working toward justice and reconciliation, individuals and communities can heal wounds, restore trust, and rebuild societies based on principles of truth, compassion, and respect for all human life.

This journey toward healing and restoration requires a commitment to ethical living and collective efforts to promote a world where peace, justice, and harmony prevail.

Doubt

Pursuing the teachings, the maintenance of doubt, contrary to a healthy pursuit of truth rooted in logic and knowledge, signifies a deficiency in perceiving and acknowledging the fundamental realities and connections that constitute truth.

Truth itself resides in the clear understanding of factual nature and effective reality.

With disciplined clarity and recognition, all traces of doubt naturally vanish as the complete reality and its fundamental truths become apparent.

Achieving this clarity requires diligent effort and evolutionary growth of consciousness.

Until one attains this clear vision and recognition through diligent personal development, doubts persist as a natural part of the quest for genuine knowledge and truth.

Doubt, then, reflects the ongoing struggle of evolving consciousness and the journey towards understanding.

However, progress demands that doubts be dispelled through acquired knowledge and acknowledged truths.

This transformative process hinges upon cultivating and applying clear vision and recognition to comprehend truth and efficacy.

The path to this understanding is challenging and fraught with doubts, which must not be suppressed forcefully or indulged without restraint.

Instead, doubts must be addressed and resolved through disciplined clarity and recognition of truth.

This journey represents a crucial evolution in consciousness, where doubt gives way to enlightenment through the pursuit and recognition of genuine knowledge and ultimate truth.

Active engagement with the external world

According to the teachings, it is important not to romanticize or overestimate the value of self-rumination and mere self-observation as something inherently profound or transformative.

Simply reflecting on oneself without purpose or direction does not inherently lead to significant progress in the evolution of consciousness.

Genuine growth in consciousness requires more than passive introspection—it necessitates active engagement, thoughtful analysis, and practical application of insights gained.

Merely dwelling on one's thoughts and experiences without a constructive purpose can lead to a sense of stagnation rather than advancement.

The misconception that self-obsession or endless rumination leads to profound insights or spiritual growth can be misleading.

True evolution of consciousness involves a balanced approach that integrates self-reflection with outward action and interaction with the world.

It requires individuals to move beyond introspection as an end in itself and to use insights gained to foster positive change and understanding.

Therefore, while introspection and self-observation can be valuable tools for personal development, they must be coupled with deliberate efforts to apply newfound insights to one's life and relationships.

This active engagement with the external world and the application of self-awareness are essential for genuine progress in the journey of consciousness evolution.

Every deed

According to the Herald, every deed can hold profound significance if an individual allows their consciousness to recognize and transform each action into a conscious understanding of reality.

The depth and impact of any deed depend on how consciously one directs their awareness, as this focus infuses each material action with a profound sense of realization, especially when the intention is to expand and evolve existing knowledge and skills.

When a person willingly and motivatedly engages in this process, they imbue each of their actions with unique and particular meaning.

This meaning is influenced by their conscious objectives and the degree of concentration applied, demonstrating that human beings can consciously create evolution with a specific aim: the recognition of true reality through the development of conscious values.

These consciousness-based values are not mere abstractions but represent significant synaptic, energetic, or consciousness-based connections within the brain.

They hold intrinsic value and lead to the understanding and application of the fundamental laws and recommendations of Creation.

Thus, by actively engaging in conscious development, individuals not only enhance their own understanding but also contribute to a greater recognition of universal principles.

This process of creating meaningful connections and applying them effectively is essential for recognizing and living by the deeper laws of existence.

Positive thoughts

As shown in the teachings, Individuals who embody clean, good, and positive thoughts and who actively reinforce these thoughts become resilient against harmful psychological influences.

The strength of their pure and positive thoughts prevents any detrimental attack, effectively shielding their psyche from harm.

Clear, clean, and neutral-positive thinking harnesses its immense power to form constructive habits from which new, healthy, and valuable ideas, wishes, and determinations continually arise.

This process has an evolutionary effect, as such thoughts foster positive development and growth.

To maintain optimal psychological and physical health and to fulfill one's potential, it is crucial to nurture consciousness.

This involves cultivating ideas and wishes that give rise to constructive thoughts, which in turn manifest and shape one's reality according to their nature.

Therefore, improving and brightening one's psyche, body, and overall appearance requires attention to maintaining consciousness and fostering life-affirming thoughts.

Negative thoughts, such as those driven by malice, envy, addiction, disappointment, and hate, as well as thoughts stemming from fear, selfishness, and unrest, have equally detrimental effects on the psyche and various aspects of life.

To promote positive outcomes, one must focus on nurturing thoughts that are affirming and life-enhancing.

The body

The body is simply a vehicle for the Creation Energy to experience life.

Its appearance, shape, or physical characteristics do not determine the true purpose of existence.

Regardless of how the body looks, the important thing is the lessons learned through the experience of living.

The evolution of Creation Energy is not concerned with how the body appears.

What matters most is the growth that comes from inhabiting a physical form and navigating the challenges of life.

The body is temporary, but the energy within it is constantly evolving through those experiences.

Once Earth's people understand this truth, they will begin to pay more attention to the evolution of their Creation Energy than to the physical form they inhabit.

They will realize that focusing on the body's appearance is a distraction from the deeper purpose of their existence.

As this awareness spreads, humanity will shift its focus toward the true meaning of life.

By valuing the lessons learned from living in a body, they will prioritize the growth of their inner energy and see the body for what it truly is—a temporary vessel for spiritual evolution.

Mount Shasta

The teachings reveal to us that Mount Shasta, located in northern California, is a venerable volcanic mountain known for its rugged terrain and challenging climbs.

Despite its formidable appearance, the mountain harbors a mysterious secret: within its depths lies a small city inhabited by descendants of extraterrestrial beings.

These inhabitants, described as a majestic and peaceful race, maintain a cautious distance from Earth humans, striving to remain concealed.

The entrance to their underground city is cleverly concealed beneath the eastern peak of the mountain, ensuring it remains undetected by outsiders.

Should humans inadvertently approach, they are subtly immobilized or distracted by advanced beam weapons carried by the city dwellers for security.

In the contact reports, you can find that the inhabitants of this hidden city are known to possess golden spherical spaceships, a testament to their advanced mastery of space travel.

These ships occasionally appear in the skies, though they typically remain hidden from human view.

Members of this race are characterized by their well-proportioned stature and distinctive features: natural blond, long, and curly hair.

Despite their shyness towards Earthlings, they occasionally venture into nearby villages to engage in secretive bartering before swiftly retreating upon sensing human presence.

According to the information in the teachings, Mount Shasta is not the sole location where this enigmatic race resides.

Early in their history, they divided into three smaller groups, with two other communities dwelling deep underground on the Aleutian Islands and in Alaska.

The total population of these beings numbers around 700 individuals, maintaining a discreet existence while navigating their interactions with the human world.

Attachment to earthly riches

It is futile to anchor one's thoughts and emotions solely to material wealth, as such pursuits do not lead to an understanding of the ultimate truth.

In keeping with the teachings, earthly riches, regardless of their magnitude or form, cannot grant access to the profound truths that transcend material existence.

Likewise, the acquisition of virtues, which are foundational to ethical living and personal growth, cannot be attained through wealth alone.

True understanding and insight into life's deeper truths require introspection, wisdom, and a commitment to moral and spiritual development.

These qualities cannot be bought or acquired through external means but are cultivated through inner reflection and ethical conduct.

Virtues such as honesty, compassion, and integrity are built upon a foundation of personal integrity and self-awareness rather than material possessions.

While material wealth may provide temporary comfort or security, its pursuit should not overshadow the quest for genuine meaning and fulfillment.

Attachment to earthly riches can distract individuals from focusing on inner growth and spiritual enlightenment.

True fulfillment comes from aligning one's thoughts and actions with universal principles of truth, justice, and compassion, which transcend the transient nature of material possessions.

In time, the pursuit of truth and virtue requires a commitment to humility, self-discipline, and a willingness to engage in meaningful introspection.

By recognizing the limitations of material wealth in fostering spiritual and moral growth, individuals can redirect their focus toward cultivating inner virtues that lead to lasting peace, fulfillment, and a deeper understanding of life's ultimate truths.

Products of human imagination

As Billy taught, all gods are constructs of human imagination, born from mistaken beliefs and cultural narratives.

These deities, worshipped and revered throughout history, are products of human interpretation and the desire to find meaning and solace in the universe.

However, there is no need for individuals to diminish themselves or seek happiness and solace from these fabricated entities.

Human beings have created gods as symbols of power, guidance, and divine intervention in times of need.

Yet, the belief in these entities as supernatural beings with authority over human destiny is a reflection of human yearning for understanding and control in a complex world.

While these beliefs may provide comfort to some, they are not necessary for finding true happiness or fulfillment.

The recognition that gods are human inventions liberates individuals from feelings of inadequacy or dependence on external forces for happiness and consolation.

It encourages self-reliance and empowers individuals to seek fulfillment through personal growth, meaningful relationships, and ethical living.

Rather than looking to imaginary gods for guidance or reassurance, individuals can cultivate their own inner strength and resilience.

Realizing the understanding that gods are products of human imagination promotes a worldview grounded in reason, compassion, and self-empowerment.

It encourages individuals to take responsibility for their own actions and decisions, fostering a sense of autonomy and agency in shaping their lives.

By focusing on personal development and fostering genuine connections with others, individuals can cultivate a sense of purpose and fulfillment that transcends the need for external validation or divine intervention.

Duty fulfillment

Those who diligently fulfill their duties and responsibilities to the best of their ability also cultivate the virtues necessary for their role in society.

In step with the creation energy teachings, by consistently meeting the expectations placed upon them, individuals develop qualities that contribute to their personal growth and effectiveness in their respective positions.

Fulfilling duties faithfully involves a commitment to reliability, accountability, and ethical conduct.

This dedication fosters virtues such as reliability as individuals strive to honor their commitments and obligations consistently.

By upholding these standards, they build trust and credibility within their communities and workplaces.

The virtues cultivated through faithful duty fulfillment vary depending on the role and responsibilities involved.

In professional settings, for example, integrity and competence are essential virtues that contribute to effective leadership and organizational success.

In personal relationships, virtues such as patience, empathy, and fairness promote harmony and mutual respect.

Finally, the process of fulfilling duties with dedication and integrity not only strengthens individual character but also enhances one's ability to contribute positively to society.

It fosters a sense of purpose and accomplishment as individuals recognize the significance of their roles in shaping a community guided by ethical principles and mutual support.

Love for truth

Virtues encompass a spectrum of qualities, each possessing its own distinct significance and value.

Among these virtues, some stand out as particularly crucial due to their fundamental role in fostering personal and societal well-being.

Foremost among them are true love, compassion for others, and dedication to truth.

Truly, in accordance with the teachings, these virtues form the bedrock of ethical living, promoting harmony and understanding in human interactions.

True love, encompassing both selfless affection and empathy for others, lies at the heart of virtuous behavior.

It encourages individuals to prioritize the well-being of others and fosters deep connections based on mutual respect and care.

Love for truth follows closely, guiding individuals to seek and uphold honesty and integrity in their thoughts and actions, thereby fostering trust and credibility.

Uprightness, equitableness, and conscientious accountability are also essential virtues that contribute to a just and balanced society.

Upholding principles of fairness and impartiality ensures that decisions and actions are guided by ethical standards and promote equity among individuals.

Conscientiousness emphasizes the importance of responsibility and diligence in fulfilling one's obligations and commitments, thereby fostering reliability and trustworthiness in personal and professional endeavors.

Modesty and courageous strength complement these virtues by promoting humility and resilience.

Modesty encourages individuals to maintain a balanced view of their abilities and achievements, fostering humility and respect for others.

Courageous strength enables individuals to confront challenges with fortitude and determination, demonstrating resilience in the face of adversity and inspiring others to persevere in the pursuit of virtuous living.

Virtues vary in significance but share the common goal of promoting ethical conduct and harmonious relationships.

True love, compassion, honesty, fairness, conscientiousness, modesty, and courage form the cornerstone of a virtuous life, guiding individuals toward personal fulfillment and contributing to a more just and compassionate society.

Embracing these virtues fosters a community where mutual respect, trust, and empathy prevail, enriching the lives of individuals and strengthening the fabric of human interaction.

Mental and bodily states

Thoughts and feelings, along with the resulting psychological state, can significantly influence physical health, affecting the onset and progression of illnesses and diseases.

For instance, healing processes can be impacted by the nature of one's thoughts and feelings.

Negative, destructive, or unhealthy thoughts tend to generate corresponding negative feelings, which then shape the psyche.

This interplay can lead to increased susceptibility to illnesses and a compromised immune system.

As we learn in the teachings, when thoughts are constructive, positive, and balanced, they foster similar positive feelings and a healthier psychological state.

This positive mindset strengthens the immune system and imbues the body with protective energy, enhancing overall health and resilience.

Thus, the quality of thoughts and feelings plays a crucial role in determining physical well-being.

The relationship between thoughts, feelings, and physical health underscores the importance of mental and emotional well-being in maintaining a healthy body.

Positive and healthy mental states contribute to better immune function and overall bodily protection, while negative mental states can lead to health challenges.

The influence of thoughts and feelings on physical health highlights the interconnection between mental and bodily states.

Constructive mental habits support a stronger immune system and greater health, whereas negative mental states can impair physical well-being.

This understanding reinforces the importance of fostering a positive and balanced mindset for optimal health.

Final moments

When a person reaches old age having lived a life of righteousness, peace, love, joy, freedom, and harmony, their later years reflect these qualities with a calm and harmonious demeanor akin to a magnificent sunset.

As outlined by the creation energy teachings, the process of dying, for such an individual, is equally serene and composed, mirroring the peaceful and balanced life they have led.

In this case, age is merely a number, and the experience of dying is as tranquil and harmonious as the life lived in alignment with positive thoughts and feelings.

The individual's thoughts and feelings, shaped by their experiences, knowledge, and wisdom, contribute to a peaceful transition at the end of their earthly existence.

Healthy, positive, and balanced thoughts of love, peace, freedom, and harmony are crucial not only for living a fulfilling life but also for ensuring a serene departure.

These thoughts shape the entire path of life and play a significant role in how one experiences the final moments.

As a person prepares to cross over into the realm of spiritual light, their final moments will reflect the peace and harmony they have cultivated throughout their life.

Selfishness

A selfish person often fails to recognize that their psychological conflicts, suffering, and injuries are self-created, not the responsibility of others.

Instead of understanding this, they project their issues onto those around them, leading them to harbor hatred and act against others.

This behavior manifests as attempts to moralize, persuade, manipulate, or dominate, aiming to control others and alleviate their own psychological distress.

In their quest to manage their own suffering and insecurity, these individuals might resort to controlling behaviors to maintain a sense of power and independence.

Their selfish desire for possessions, profit, and wealth further drives them to exert control over others, believing that such dominance will alleviate their own internal conflicts.

As they accumulate wealth, power, or a higher worldly position, their desire for control can intensify.

This can evolve into an unhealthy obsession with domination, where the pursuit of absolute authority becomes paramount.

The individual's need to exert power often reflects a deeper insecurity and inability to address their own issues.

The selfish person's actions are a reflection of their own unresolved psychological conflicts.

Their attempts to dominate and manipulate others are not only driven by personal insecurity but also by a relentless pursuit of material gain and control.

This behavior underscores their failure to understand that the true resolution of their inner turmoil cannot come from controlling others but must be addressed within themselves.

Selfishness II

As the teachings continue, a selfish person often fails to recognize that their psychological conflicts, suffering, and injuries are self-created, not the responsibility of others.

Instead of understanding this, they project their issues onto those around them, leading them to harbor hatred and act against others.

This behavior manifests as attempts to moralize, persuade, manipulate, or dominate, aiming to control others and alleviate their own psychological distress.

In their quest to manage their own suffering and insecurity, these individuals might resort to controlling behaviors to maintain a sense of power and independence.

Their selfish desire for possessions, profit, and wealth further drives them to exert control over others, believing that such dominance will alleviate their own internal conflicts.

As they accumulate wealth, power, or a higher worldly position, their desire for control can intensify.

This can evolve into an unhealthy obsession with domination, where the pursuit of absolute authority becomes paramount.

The individual's need to exert power often reflects a deeper insecurity and inability to address their own issues.

Truly, the selfish person's actions are a reflection of their own unresolved psychological conflicts.

Their attempts to dominate and manipulate others are not only driven by personal insecurity but also by a relentless pursuit of material gain and control.

This behavior underscores their failure to understand that the true resolution of their inner turmoil cannot come from controlling others but must be addressed within themselves.

Genuine love

As stated in the teachings, those who cultivate genuine love within themselves and safeguard it experience inner peace and freedom, which extends outwardly into their interactions with others.

True love, nurtured and preserved, forms a foundation of emotional stability and fulfillment, allowing individuals to navigate life with a sense of tranquility and authenticity.

Internally, fostering genuine love promotes a deep sense of contentment and emotional resilience.

It provides individuals with a source of strength and comfort, enabling them to approach challenges with grace and empathy.

This inner peace radiates outward, influencing their relationships and interactions with others and fostering an environment of mutual respect and understanding.

Externally, those who embody true love seek harmony in their interactions with the world.

They strive to create connections based on empathy and compassion, contributing positively to their communities and society at large.

Their actions reflect a commitment to fostering unity and cooperation, bridging divides, and promoting a collective sense of well-being.

The continuous pursuit of harmony becomes a guiding principle for individuals who value and uphold true love in their lives.

They actively seek to align their thoughts, emotions, and actions with principles of compassion and integrity, fostering a harmonious balance between personal fulfillment and communal unity.

In doing so, they contribute to a world where peace, freedom, and harmony prevail as guiding principles of human interaction and coexistence.

Neglect not

While it is important to care for and appreciate the body, we must not overlook the cultivation of consciousness.

Life's true purpose lies in expanding and refining our inner awareness, as this is what leads to genuine evolution.

Our bodies serve as temporary vessels for Creation Energy to express itself and evolve, but they are not our ultimate selves.

Therefore, while we can love our physical form, the greater love and attention must be directed inward, toward the growth of our consciousness.

Authentic self-love begins within and radiates outward.

It is not dependent on external appearances but on a true understanding of our worth, regardless of how we look.

When our love for ourselves comes from within, it frees us from superficial concerns and judgments.

How we see ourselves on the inside, with acceptance and clarity, is what truly shapes our self-worth and purpose.

It is time we shift our focus from outward appearances to the evolution of our inner being.

In a world that often emphasizes physical beauty, we risk losing sight of what truly matters—the development of our consciousness.

By prioritizing inner growth, we foster a sense of purpose and value that transcends the temporary nature of our bodies.

This shift allows us to embrace a deeper form of fulfillment that is lasting and meaningful.

Ultimately, by placing our attention on the growth of consciousness, we align ourselves with the true purpose of existence.

This path toward inner evolution enriches our lives and connects us to Creation.

As we focus on our inner selves, we cultivate a sense of peace and authenticity that benefits not only ourselves but also the greater whole.

This journey inward is the path to true fulfillment and self-acceptance.

Following the truth

Following the truth not only benefits your own well-being but also contributes to the well-being of all humankind.

In agreement with the teachings, truth serves as a guiding principle that facilitates peace, freedom, love, and harmony within yourself and in your interactions with others.

It aligns your thoughts, feelings, and actions with ethical integrity and clarity, fostering a sense of inner coherence and external unity.

Achieving personal peace and freedom through truth involves living authentically and in accordance with principles that uphold honesty and fairness.

By embracing truth, individuals cultivate inner tranquility and resilience, enabling them to navigate life's challenges with grace and integrity.

This inner peace extends to relationships, promoting mutual respect and understanding among fellow human beings.

Love and harmony flourish when truth forms the foundation of interactions and connections with others.

Genuine connections are forged through empathy, compassion, and sincerity, fostering meaningful relationships built on trust and mutual support.

Truthful communication promotes openness and vulnerability, strengthening interpersonal bonds and nurturing a sense of community and belonging.

At the end, embracing truth as a guiding principle leads to holistic well-being for oneself and humanity at large.

It encourages individuals to strive for ethical living and moral responsibility, creating a ripple effect of positive influence that contributes to a more compassionate and harmonious world.

By embodying truth in thought, word, and deed, individuals not only enhance their own lives but also contribute positively to the collective evolution of humankind toward greater peace, freedom, and love.

The state of the psyche

As the teachings show, consciousness plays a crucial role in determining its own health through intelligent and rational thought.

It exerts significant influence over the state of the body, impacting its health or decline, again primarily through the power of thought.

Central to this process is the state of the psyche, which is shaped by various feelings rooted in corresponding thoughts.

Consequently, the overall health and vitality of the body can vary based on the condition of the psyche, leading to either wellness and strength or illness and weakness.

However, it is essential to clarify that not all diseases and physical ailments are solely the result of thoughts, feelings, or psychological states.

While the psyche can affect physical health, many illnesses and conditions arise from factors unrelated to mental or emotional states.

These diseases often develop due to other underlying causes that do not directly connect with the realm of thoughts, feelings, or psychological conditions.

Thus, although there is a significant interplay between consciousness and physical health, it is important to recognize that the manifestation and impact of many physical ailments can occur independently of psychological factors.

Understanding this distinction helps in addressing health issues more comprehensively.

While the psyche and thoughts can influence bodily health, following the teachings, it is crucial to acknowledge that numerous diseases and conditions emerge from different sources.

This nuanced understanding ensures a more accurate approach to both mental and physical health care.

Truthful living

As outlined in the teachings, the pursuit of truth is essential for fostering love and wisdom, which in turn nurture harmony, peace, and freedom within oneself and in interactions with others.

Truth serves as a guiding light that illuminates paths toward understanding and empathy, enabling individuals to cultivate deeper connections and mutual respect.

Love, rooted in genuine understanding and compassion, flourishes when grounded in truth.

It transcends superficiality and fosters authentic relationships built on trust and mutual appreciation.

Wisdom, derived from the discernment of truth, empowers individuals to make informed decisions and navigate life's complexities with clarity and insight.

Consonance, or harmony, emerges naturally when individuals align their actions and beliefs with the truth.

It fosters a sense of coherence and unity, both internally within one's thoughts and values and externally in relationships and communities.

This alignment cultivates an environment where conflicts are resolved peacefully and cooperation thrives.

Peace and freedom blossom as direct consequences of living in accordance with truth, love, and wisdom.

Truthful living promotes inner tranquility and equanimity, shielding individuals from internal turmoil and external pressures.

It also empowers individuals to embrace their authentic selves and pursue aspirations without fear of contradiction or compromise.

In essence, embracing truth as a guiding principle fosters a life enriched with love, wisdom, consonance, peace, and freedom.

It lays the foundation for personal fulfillment and harmonious relationships, fostering a positive ripple effect that extends beyond individual lives to create a more compassionate and enlightened society.

The act of believing

Belief should not be confused with virtue; rather, it is a form of longing or desire directed towards something perceived as capable of being supplicated, revered, and offering assistance.

According to the teachings, this belief often centers around an imagined entity that is considered invisible and entirely devoid of power or capability to cause harm or confer benefits.

The act of believing involves placing trust or faith in an intangible entity that is presumed to hold influence over certain aspects of life.

However, this entity remains a fictional construct, lacking the ability to manifest tangible outcomes or affect real-world events positively or negatively.

Those who hold beliefs in such entities often attribute qualities of guidance, protection, or intervention to them despite the absence of evidence supporting their existence or impact.

This belief can serve as a psychological comfort or a source of perceived meaning and order in an otherwise uncertain world.

While belief may provide individuals with a sense of spiritual connection or purpose, it should not be equated with virtue.

True virtue lies in the cultivation of ethical principles, moral integrity, and compassionate actions that contribute positively to personal growth and the well-being of others in tangible and meaningful ways.

A true friendship

A true friendship is characterized by deep empathy and understanding between individuals.

As the teachings show, this empathy is essential for fostering a connection where both parties genuinely care for one another, sharing not only their thoughts and feelings but also their experiences and challenges with honesty and sincerity.

Such a relationship requires a foundation of honest, affectionate communication and mutual respect.

Effective, true friendships are built on sincere love and positive, meaningful interactions.

It is crucial that the individuals involved engage in genuine, constructive exchanges rather than relying on abstract or exaggerated notions of what friendship should be.

Clear, thoughtful, and realistic decisions about the relationship help maintain its integrity and depth.

Additionally, a strong friendship demands proactive and constructive conflict management.

To maintain a healthy relationship, it is important to address potential disputes before they escalate.

This involves both parties being committed to a process of guided mediation, where disagreements are resolved through open communication and mutual understanding.

A successful friendship involves reaching a mutually acceptable consensus or agreement.

This collaborative approach ensures that both individuals are equally satisfied and that the relationship remains robust and fulfilling.

By following these principles, friends can nurture a bond that is both resilient and deeply rewarding.

The journey of self-education

Every human being has the capacity to acquire virtues, and indeed, it is their responsibility to actively cultivate their character and virtues throughout their lives.

Indeed, based on the teachings, this ongoing process of self-education and personal discipline is essential for moral and ethical development.

It involves not only acquiring knowledge but also embodying virtues through deliberate practice and reflection.

The acquisition of virtues requires individuals to engage in continuous self-improvement and learning.

It entails nurturing qualities such as integrity, compassion, resilience, and wisdom, which contribute to a well-rounded and virtuous character.

This journey of self-education involves introspection, learning from experiences, and consciously aligning one's actions with ethical principles.

Central to the cultivation of virtues is the recognition that personal growth is a lifelong endeavor.

Human beings are tasked with perpetually refining their character and behavior, adapting to new challenges and evolving moral landscapes.

This ongoing commitment to self-education ensures that individuals remain engaged in the pursuit of excellence and ethical integrity throughout their lives.

The process of forming virtues through personal discipline encompasses various aspects of life, including moral reasoning, emotional intelligence, and social responsibility.

It requires individuals to develop a deep understanding of ethical values and principles, applying them in both personal interactions and broader societal contexts.

By welcoming this journey of self-education, individuals not only enhance their own well-being but also contribute positively to the moral fabric of their communities.

Ultimately, the lifelong pursuit of virtue is a testament to human potential and resilience.

It underscores the innate capacity of individuals to grow, learn, and adapt in pursuit of ethical excellence.

By embracing personal discipline and continuous self-education, human beings empower themselves to lead meaningful lives guided by principles of integrity, compassion, and moral responsibility.

The inner world of consciousness

The inner world of consciousness serves as the fertile ground from which thoughts emerge, giving rise to feelings that shape the psyche of human beings.

Consistent with the teachings, It is within this internal realm that individuals must mold their character, virtues, and unique personality.

This process is guided by the principles and directives inherent in the laws and recommendations of Creation, providing a framework for ethical living and personal development.

Thoughts, originating from the depths of consciousness, hold the power to influence emotions and perceptions.

These emotional responses, in turn, contribute to the formation of one's psyche—the complex amalgamation of beliefs, values, and mental frameworks that define an individual's inner life.

Through conscious awareness and introspection, people navigate their thoughts and emotions, striving to align their actions with the ethical guidelines prescribed by universal truths.

The cultivation of character and virtues is an ongoing journey shaped by the interplay of thoughts, feelings, and conscious choices.

By adhering to the guidelines set forth by the laws of Creation, individuals forge a path toward moral integrity and personal fulfillment.

This alignment with universal principles fosters a sense of harmony within oneself and with the larger cosmos, promoting a balanced and purposeful existence.

The integration of these principles into daily life fosters a harmonious relationship between individual consciousness and the broader cosmic order.

It encourages individuals to embody virtues such as compassion, wisdom, and integrity, enhancing not only their personal growth but also their contribution to a more enlightened and ethical society.

The dynamic power of action

As asserted in the teachings, to fully grasp the profound truth revealed through the laws and recommendations inherent in the creation of all things, it is insufficient to merely follow natural abilities and cultivated virtues dutifully.

True understanding of this truth demands something more: the dynamic power of action derived from the creative force inherent in human beings.

This power, known as spirit-form, imbues individuals with consciousness, psyche, thoughts, and feelings, animating their inner world and guiding their actions.

Human beings are animated not solely by innate capabilities or learned virtues but also by natural and potent energy sourced from their spiritual essence.

This creative and animating force, referred to as spirit-creational energy, emanates from the core of their being, shaping their existence and driving their engagement with the world.

It is through this energy that individuals manifest their inner potential and navigate the complexities of life with purpose and vitality.

Understanding and harnessing this spirit-creational energy is essential for aligning with the deeper truths of existence.

It empowers individuals to transcend mere compliance with external laws and expectations, enabling them to embody authenticity and integrity in their thoughts, actions, and interactions.

This profound connection to their creative power allows them to live in harmony with the universal principles that govern all creation, fostering a life guided by wisdom, compassion, and spiritual fulfillment.

Indeed, embracing and channeling the spirit-creational energy within oneself unlocks a deeper understanding of truth and purpose.

It represents a transformative journey towards self-discovery and alignment with the natural order, enriching not only personal growth but also contributing positively to the collective evolution of humanity.

The key

Human beings on Earth have not yet fully understood their true nature.

They continue to perceive themselves merely as physical entities composed of flesh and bones. This limited view prevents them from recognizing a deeper reality.

In truth, humans are comprised of a fundamental creative energy that links them to the universal consciousness.

This connection implies that they are more than just physical forms; they are integral parts of a larger, interconnected whole.

Furthermore, human beings possess the remarkable ability to shape their own lives through the power of their thoughts.

This capability stems from their inherent connection to the universal energy, which influences their experiences and reality.

By acknowledging and accepting this connection, individuals can harness the power of their minds to create the life they envision.

This realization holds the potential to transform their understanding of themselves and the world around them.

Continuous dedication

In line with the creation energy teachings, persistent practice cultivates proficiency and builds strength and mastery.

Those who habituate themselves to consistently engaging in truthful and reliable actions through practice will effortlessly, joyfully, and confidently perform virtuous deeds.

Such individuals embody a natural ease and certainty in their actions, embodying a character enriched with virtue and goodness.

Through continuous dedication to truthful and infallible practices, individuals not only enhance their capabilities but also nurture a sense of inner strength and competence.

This commitment allows them to approach challenges with grace and assurance, fostering a mindset that embraces virtuous conduct as a natural extension of their being.

Their actions resonate with authenticity and integrity, reflecting a deep-seated commitment to living in harmony with ethical principles.

The path to proficiency and mastery lies in the steadfast pursuit of truth and reliability through diligent practice.

By understanding this journey, individuals not only enhance their own abilities but also contribute positively to the world around them, embodying virtues that inspire and uplift others.

The focus of mourning

In harmony with the teachings, the focus of mourning should not be directed toward those who have passed away but instead toward the living individuals who remain unaware, lacking in wisdom, devoid of love, and constrained by a lack of freedom and peace.

These individuals live their lives in a state of ignorance, detached from the profound essence of their existence.

They are entangled in conflicts that obscure the true purpose of life, perpetuating disharmony within themselves and their surroundings.

The lamentable state of these individuals lies not in their physical existence but in their spiritual and emotional disconnection from deeper truths.

Their lives are marked by a pervasive ignorance that blinds them to the richness of wisdom and the transformative power of love.

They are shackled by limitations that restrict their freedom to explore and embrace the full spectrum of human experience, leaving them bereft of inner peace and harmony.

In mourning these living souls, we acknowledge their profound struggle with identity and purpose.

Their plight is a reflection of broader societal challenges where material pursuits overshadow spiritual growth and communal well-being.

It is a call to recognize and address the underlying causes of their discontent and disillusionment, offering avenues for healing and restoration.

By directing our mourning towards the living who grapple with ignorance, lack of wisdom, lovelessness, and inner turmoil, we affirm our commitment to fostering a more compassionate and enlightened society.

Through empathy, education, and a renewed focus on spiritual growth, we endeavor to awaken individuals to the true essence of their existence and guide them toward a life filled with meaning, freedom, and profound peace.

Evolving awareness

The human brain operates with absolute logic and consistency in its lawful processes. Through its balanced and neutral transformation, it aligns with the eternal pattern of creational-spiritual energy, which it can then consciously utilize and assess.

This alignment is an indisputable fact available to every individual, achievable through the conscious use of their thoughts and feelings to gain deeper knowledge.

In practical terms, following the teachings means that as a person navigates through life, they encounter different symbols representing various aspects of their experience.

For example, when walking along a dirt road, they may see a certain path ahead, symbolizing the present moment and a destination further off, representing their future goals and visions.

The past, though present behind them, is not visible unless they choose to remember or reflect on it.

Thus, individuals consciously engage the past, present, and future as part of their ongoing development and evolution of consciousness.

By focusing on the present and future while understanding the past only as a reference point, individuals can align their actions and decisions with their evolving awareness.

This approach allows humans to effectively use their consciousness to progress and grow, consciously integrating past experiences with current realities and future aspirations.

In doing so, they harmonize their awareness with the broader creational-spiritual patterns and continue their journey of evolution.

Self sabotaging

In their attempt to shield themselves from self-criticism, people choose to ridicule their own aspirations and longings.

According to Billy, this unconventional approach inadvertently creates fertile ground for lovelessness, where genuine affection and empathy struggle to flourish.

By belittling their own hopes and desires, they inadvertently nurture a sense of emotional bondage, constraining their capacity to experience true freedom and fulfillment.

This self-deprecating attitude not only hampers their personal peace but also perpetuates a cycle of inner discord and dissatisfaction.

Moreover, this mockery of their own aspirations serves to entrench inequality within their inner being.

By devaluing their own dreams and ambitions, they may unknowingly reinforce a hierarchy within themselves where certain desires or goals are deemed unworthy or unattainable.

This internalized inequality can lead to a fragmented sense of self, where parts of their identity are dismissed or marginalized, hindering their ability to achieve holistic self-acceptance and harmony.

By avoiding genuine self-reflection and resorting to self-mockery, individuals risk fostering an environment within themselves where love, peace, and equality struggle to take root and flourish.

Accepting self-awareness and compassionately engaging with their own hopes and desires can pave the way towards a more integrated and harmonious inner life, fostering greater emotional well-being and fulfillment.

Insights gained to effect

Contemplating one's existence excessively without purpose or direction can impede personal growth and the evolution of consciousness.

As the teachings tell us, when individuals dwell excessively on self-reflection without taking meaningful action, they risk stagnation rather than progress.

The journey towards higher consciousness requires active engagement with the world and introspection that leads to constructive change.

Merely turning inward without purposeful reflection can be counterproductive, preventing individuals from ascending to higher levels of awareness and understanding.

In the pursuit of evolution, it is crucial to strike a balance between introspection and outward action.

Self-reflection should serve as a tool for gaining insights and understanding one's place in the broader scheme of existence.

However, when rumination becomes an end in itself, it becomes a hindrance rather than a catalyst for personal and spiritual development.

True growth involves not only deep introspection but also applying insights gained to effect positive changes in oneself and in interactions with others.

Moreover, excessive rumination can lead to a cycle of self-absorption that isolates individuals from the world around them. It can foster a sense of detachment or disconnection from meaningful experiences and relationships.

To ascend in consciousness is to cultivate awareness not only of oneself but also of the interconnectedness with others and the environment.

It requires a holistic approach that integrates self-awareness with empathy, compassion, and active participation in the unfolding of life.

The path to higher consciousness involves transcending the limitations imposed by aimless rumination.

It demands embracing a dynamic process of self-discovery, learning, and growth that enriches both personal development and collective evolution.

By channeling introspection into constructive actions and meaningful engagement with the world, individuals can foster a deeper understanding of themselves and contribute positively to the evolution of consciousness.

Recording device

A human being is like a recording device that functions only during life.

When life ends, both the tape and the recording come to a stop, and the memories tied to that existence fade away.

The experiences and knowledge acquired during a lifetime are transferred from the material consciousness to the Creation Energy upon death.

However, as we take our final breath and close our eyes for the last time, rest assured they will open once more in a new life.

In this fresh existence, we have no memory of the past because a new human being emerges with a new material consciousness and personality.

It is as if a blank tape is set, ready to record new experiences.

Each new life comes into being completely separate from the last, with no connection between the new consciousness and the former one.

Every time life is animated by the Creation Energy, it is distinct and unlinked from what came before.

This ongoing cycle of renewal and growth allows us to continually evolve.

Though the memories of past lives are erased, the wisdom and knowledge acquired remain within the subconscious mind, ready to be drawn upon by the human being.

The essence of who we are endures through these cycles of life and rebirth.

Each new existence offers the chance to learn, grow, and transform.

When a human being truly understands their eternal nature, feelings such as envy, jealousy, and fear fall away, replaced by the deeper realization of their timeless presence in the flow of life.

Managing the origin of thoughts

Just as the physical body requires pure and healthy nourishment to thrive and remain largely free from suffering and illness, thoughts also need pure, healthy, and positive nourishment to flourish.

In conformity with the teachings, positive thoughts emerge when they are originally free, open, peaceful, and harmonious, thus remaining neutral and balanced.

Thoughts cannot be altered merely by adopting a new diet, engaging in sports, extensive talking, or acquiring book knowledge.

Instead, they can only be changed by deeply understanding and analyzing them to shape and use them constructively and creatively.

This process involves allowing thoughts to exert their own positive influence through their inherent power.

When thoughts are initially formed in a positive and balanced state, individuals are less likely to be swayed by negative factors and desires.

The origin of thoughts is influenced by a variety of factors, including ideas, views, wishes, desires, and life experiences, which evoke emotional responses that impact subsequent thoughts.

Therefore, it is essential to manage the origin of thoughts to ensure they are formed and directed in a manner that promotes health, purity, and positivity.

By controlling the root of thoughts, one can ensure that their power only manifests what is truly healthy, good, and constructive.

Unlike apes

As stated in the teachings, human beings must not resemble apes or those who are despised due to their misconduct.

Unlike apes, humans are accountable for their own actions, deeds, thoughts, and feelings.

This fundamental responsibility distinguishes humans from other beings and emphasizes the importance of self-awareness and ethical conduct.

Recognizing this distinction is crucial in daily life.

It prompts individuals to reflect on their choices and behaviors, striving to uphold integrity and moral values.

By taking personal accountability seriously, people cultivate a sense of dignity and contribute positively to society.

Furthermore, this awareness encourages empathy and understanding towards others.

It fosters a culture of mutual respect and cooperation, where individuals support each other in striving for moral excellence and personal growth.

Therefore, embrace your unique capacity for accountability and ethical behavior. Let it guide you in making decisions that reflect your values and principles.

By doing so, you not only uphold your own dignity but also contribute to a more harmonious and compassionate world.

The principles imparted by Creation

It is advised through the teachings to adhere steadfastly to the principles imparted by Creation and natural laws.

Remembering and respecting these principles ensures that wrong thoughts, emotions, and actions do not lead to unnecessary hardships.

By honoring these principles, individuals align themselves with the natural order of the universe.

This alignment promotes balance, harmony, and well-being, both for oneself and for the broader community.

It encourages responsible stewardship of the Earth and fosters respect for all living beings.

Reflecting on and integrating these teachings into daily life can prevent conflicts, misunderstandings, and environmental degradation.

It encourages mindfulness and conscientious decision-making, guiding individuals toward actions that promote justice, compassion, and sustainability.

Therefore, hold fast to the wisdom imparted by Creation and natural principles.

Let these teachings guide your thoughts, emotions, and actions, ensuring a path of harmony and fulfillment.

By doing so, you contribute to a world where respect for life and the environment flourishes, benefiting present and future generations alike.

With grace and fortitude

Those who possess true knowledge of the principles of Creation and live their lives in accordance with these laws will be rewarded with joy, love, peace, freedom, harmony, and wisdom.

In conformity with the teachings, their steadfast adherence to these principles ensures that they face life and death without fear, and their sorrows are tempered by resilience and understanding.

Living in harmony with the laws of Creation fosters a sense of unity with the natural world and with fellow human beings.

It promotes inner peace and a profound connection to the universe, transcending mundane fears and anxieties.

Such individuals embody compassion and empathy, enriching their lives and the lives of those around them.

By aligning their actions with the principles of Creation, they contribute positively to the well-being of society and the planet.

Their commitment to truth and righteousness guides them through challenges with grace and fortitude, ensuring that their sorrows do not overwhelm them but instead strengthen their resolve.

In essence, embracing the wisdom of Creation leads to a life filled with purpose, contentment, and spiritual fulfillment.

It allows individuals to navigate life's complexities with wisdom and compassion, fostering a world where peace and harmony flourish.

Perpetuating torment

Many individuals bring misery and disgrace upon themselves by perpetuating torment and violence, burdening themselves with their own anger.

Following Billy's words, throughout history, their stubbornness and defiance have led them to reject the laws and guidance of Creation, disregarding wisdom and choosing instead to harm true prophets and messengers.

In their obstinacy and aggression, they sow discord and suffering, forsaking the principles of peace and compassion that underpin universal harmony.

By opposing those who advocate for truth and righteousness, they perpetuate cycles of conflict and division, causing harm not only to others but also to themselves.

It is essential to reflect on the consequences of such actions and embrace humility and understanding.

By honoring the principles of Creation and respecting the wisdom imparted by Billy's teachings, we can cultivate a world where justice, compassion, and mutual respect prevail.

Let us strive to build communities founded on harmony and reconciliation, rejecting violence and embracing the values that promote the well-being of all.

Prioritize integrity

As outlined in the teachings, those lacking fairness or responsibility are the ones who confuse the truth with lies.

By engaging in deceit, they inflict lasting harm upon themselves.

Their falsehoods lead to isolation, as they are surrounded only by false friends who tell them what they wish to hear.

True equitableness entails honesty and integrity in discerning and upholding the truth.

It involves seeking genuine understanding and acknowledging the consequences of one's actions.

Conversely, those who distort reality for personal gain or validation compromise their own well-being and relationships.

Therefore, prioritize integrity and authenticity in all interactions.

Embrace the truth, even when it is difficult, and surround yourself with individuals who value honesty and respect.

By cultivating genuine friendships and upholding ethical principles, you foster a supportive environment conducive to personal growth and mutual trust.

Introspection

The majority of people refuse to acknowledge or accept the truth unless they can physically grasp it, see it with their own eyes, or hear it with their ears.

However, the essence of real truth transcends physical senses; it lies in inner cognition, rationality, intellect, genuine knowledge, and wisdom that are devoid of mere beliefs.

As the teachings stated, true understanding requires introspection and intellectual inquiry, not solely relying on tangible evidence.

It involves cultivating rational thought and discernment to discern what is real and what is illusion.

Wisdom emerges from a deep exploration of ideas, principles, and experiences, free from the limitations of rigid beliefs.

To accept the real truth is to embrace a mindset open to continuous learning and growth.

It means questioning assumptions, challenging preconceived notions, and seeking deeper insights beyond surface appearances.

By nurturing a spirit of intellectual curiosity and humility, individuals can uncover profound truths that enrich their understanding of themselves and the world around them.

Therefore, let us strive for a deeper understanding of truth that transcends physical perceptions.

Let us cultivate rationality, intellect, and wisdom that are grounded in genuine knowledge and free from the constraints of narrow beliefs.

In doing so, we pave the way for personal and collective enlightenment, fostering a more enlightened and compassionate world.

Foster understanding

It is undeniable that instead of appreciating each day of peace, humanity continues to perpetrate death, devastation, and destruction in the name of imaginary gods who preach love yet paradoxically demand punishment, death, and annihilation.

As asserted by Billy, this contradiction highlights the profound consequences of misguided beliefs and actions driven by fanaticism and extremism.

The misuse of religious or ideological doctrines to justify violence undermines the very principles of compassion, tolerance, and harmony that they profess.

Rather than invoking hatred and division, true spirituality and morality should promote empathy, reconciliation, and the preservation of life.

It is essential to challenge and reject ideologies that distort sacred teachings to justify violence and oppression.

As individuals and communities, we must strive to foster understanding, respect diversity, and work toward peaceful coexistence.

By promoting dialogue, education, and mutual respect, we can build bridges across differences and create a world where love and compassion triumph over hatred and destruction.

Let us reflect on the need to embrace peace and reject violence in all its forms.

Let us honor each day of peace by promoting justice, empathy, and understanding, thereby building a world where humanity's shared values of love, compassion, and respect guide our actions and aspirations.

Throughout history

Throughout history, humanity has longed for a world defined by peace and harmony.

This enduring desire is now coming closer to realization, led by the profound wisdom of Billy Meier, the proclaimer of the New Age.

Through the Creation Energy Teachings, a new era is being ushered in, offering an unprecedented opportunity for humanity to play an active role in this transformation.

The times we are living in are truly remarkable filled with the potential for positive change.

However, this transformative shift will not come without challenges.

Humanity is set to face a series of trials born from our own actions and decisions.

As Billy Meier has foretold, these tribulations are an essential part of our journey toward a more peaceful and enlightened future.

The consequences of our behavior must be confronted and understood before we can fully embrace the new era that is emerging.

The Creation Energy Teachings provide a pathway for individuals to align themselves with the universal laws of life and creation.

These teachings emphasize personal responsibility, inner growth, and the cultivation of wisdom as the means to achieve lasting peace.

By understanding these principles, humanity can foster deeper connections with the world and one another, creating a foundation for global harmony.

As we move toward this new era, we are presented with a unique opportunity to contribute to the transformation of humanity.

The vision of a peaceful world is within our reach, but it requires that we face our past actions, learn from them, and grow as individuals.

The journey may be challenging, but it holds the promise of a better, more harmonious future.

Learn from history's lessons

Reflect on the distant past when powerful leaders made deceitful promises that wars would cease, yet countless human lives have since been sacrificed to the relentless horrors of conflict and the devastating consequences it brings.

These broken pledges serve as a stark reminder of the enduring cycle of violence and the profound impact it has on communities worldwide.

The scars of war linger long after battles cease, leaving behind widespread suffering, destruction, and loss.

In accordance with the teachings, let us learn from history's lessons and commit ourselves to seeking peaceful resolutions to conflicts.

By holding leaders accountable and advocating for diplomacy, cooperation, and reconciliation, we can strive to prevent future bloodshed and ensure a safer, more just world for all.

Honoring the memory of those who have perished in wars requires a steadfast commitment to promoting peace and understanding among nations.

Together, we can work towards a future where dialogue and compassion prevail over conflict and suffering.

Dwelling on pain

To facilitate true healing, one must abstain from direct intervention with a wound.

Persistent meddling with a healing wound disrupts its inherent restorative process and may invite complications.

The body's intrinsic capacity for self-repair is most effective when undisturbed, ensuring a more harmonious recovery.

Likewise, emotional wounds require a similar detachment, allowing the natural process of healing to unfold unobstructed.

Humans often find a peculiar satisfaction in experiencing pain, which can lead them to indulge in self-pity.

This behavior, while seemingly comforting, can be detrimental.

By focusing on their suffering, individuals may seek validation or sympathy from others, but this approach only reinforces their pain and obstructs their recovery.

Emotional pain, much like physical pain, can deeply impact both the psyche and the immune system.

When individuals dwell on their pain, it can trigger a cycle of negative thoughts and emotions, ultimately weakening their overall health.

Chronic stress and emotional distress are known to have adverse effects on the body's ability to fight off illness and recover from injuries.

It is essential to recognize that dwelling on pain can have serious implications for one's well-being.

Instead of focusing on what is lost and cannot be reclaimed, it is more productive to direct attention toward the present and seek new, positive experiences.

Thoughts of lost loved ones, though natural, should not dominate one's mental landscape.

By letting go of these memories and concentrating on current opportunities, individuals can move forward and find peace, facilitating both emotional and physical healing.

Urgent need for peace

In accordance with the teachings, It is crucial to remember the immense suffering inflicted upon countless individuals worldwide due to conflicts, crimes, and acts of violence.

Wars devastate communities, leading to the tragic loss of sons and fathers on the battlefield and the horrifying victimization of daughters and mothers through rape and murder.

Such atrocities underscore the urgent need for peace, justice, and compassion in our global community.

The profound human toll of these acts demands collective efforts to promote understanding, tolerance, and reconciliation.

By remembering the pain and devastation caused by warfare and criminality, we reaffirm our commitment to building a world where all individuals can live free from fear and violence.

Let us honor the memory of those who have suffered by working tirelessly to prevent future conflicts, promote human rights, and foster dialogue and cooperation among nations.

Together, we can strive towards a future where peace and harmony prevail, ensuring that every person's dignity and well-being are safeguarded.

Beware of falsehood

In line with the energy teachings, beware of falsehood, for it can never replace or advocate for genuine truth.

It holds no authority or ability to redeem, as it only takes away and causes destruction.

The pursuit of truth is essential, as it alone offers clarity, understanding, and genuine solutions. Falsehood, on the other hand, obscures reality and leads to misguided actions and outcomes.

It undermines trust and integrity, eroding the foundations of relationships and societies.

Therefore, prioritize discernment and critical thinking in discerning truth from falsehood.

Seek knowledge and wisdom that illuminate the path forward with honesty and integrity.

By upholding the principles of truth, you contribute to a world where authenticity and trustworthiness prevail, fostering genuine progress and harmony.

Lying

Lying disrupts peace and harmony, both within ourselves and in our relationships with others.

When a person lies, they evade their own responsibility and fail to authentically present themselves.

This not only creates an unfair dynamic toward others, but it is also an injustice to the self, denying personal growth and genuine connections.

Living a life based on lies creates a heavy burden for the individual.

The constant need to maintain falsehoods leaves the mind uneasy, preventing the person from achieving inner peace.

Without peace of mind, clarity of thought is lost, making it harder to make honest decisions and act authentically.

Choosing to live truthfully brings about a sense of inner peace.

When a person is honest with themselves and others, they free themselves from the strain of deception.

This openness not only benefits the individual but also ensures that their actions align with their true feelings, reducing the likelihood of surprising or hurting others with unexpected behaviors.

Indeed, the decision to be truthful creates a life of harmony and balance.

By always speaking one's mind and embracing honesty, the individual establishes trust and consistency in their relationships and with themselves.

Choosing not to lie becomes a path toward self-respect, integrity, and peace.

Uphold a spirit of humility and gratitude

Consistent with the teachings, always cherish and remember the kindness and good deeds offered to you by your fellow human beings, past and present. Never elevate yourselves above them in pride or arrogance.

Acknowledge and appreciate the generosity and compassion shown by others.

Whether through small acts of kindness or significant contributions, these deeds enrich our lives and strengthen the bonds of our shared humanity.

By valuing the efforts of others, we cultivate a culture of gratitude and mutual respect.

Avoid the temptation to judge or criticize others from a position of superiority.

Instead, embrace humility and empathy in your interactions.

Recognize that every individual has their own strengths and struggles and that each person's contributions, however modest they may seem, contribute to the fabric of our collective existence.

In essence, uphold a spirit of humility and gratitude towards your fellow human beings.

Remember and honor the good deeds they have bestowed upon you, fostering a community where appreciation and compassion thrive.

By doing so, you contribute to a world where kindness and solidarity prevail.

One's inner world

As set forth in the creation energy teachings, true assistance comes through insight and patience, qualities that require inner richness and a commitment to truth, love, knowledge, and wisdom rather than mere compliance.

Genuine help emerges from understanding the deeper complexities of situations and exercising patience in navigating them.

It necessitates a profound connection with one's inner world—a realm of consciousness that transcends superficial responses.

This depth allows individuals to approach challenges with clarity and empathy, fostering meaningful solutions that address root causes rather than surface symptoms.

Walking the path of truth, love, knowledge, and wisdom empowers individuals to offer assistance that is informed and compassionate.

It entails a dedication to seeking understanding, embracing patience, and acting with integrity and empathy.

Through these virtues, one can navigate complexities with resilience and contribute positively to the well-being of others and society as a whole.

Therefore, cultivate inner richness through a commitment to truth and wisdom.

Approach challenges with patience and insight, ensuring that your actions are guided by genuine empathy and a deep understanding of the human experience.

In doing so, you contribute authentically to the betterment of the world around you.

Demonstrate empathy and generosity

The principles of Creation mandate a commitment to seeking knowledge, wisdom, and truth.

As disclosed by Billy, they emphasize not bowing down to fellow humans or any deities but instead showing compassion by assisting those in need with appropriate generosity.

These principles guide individuals to prioritize understanding and insight, fostering a path toward enlightenment and clarity.

They discourage submission to human authority or mythical beings, advocating instead for a focus on humanitarian efforts and support for the disadvantaged.

By upholding these principles, one embraces a noble responsibility to advance personal growth and contribute positively to society.

This entails promoting justice, compassion, and equity, ensuring that assistance is provided where it is most needed.

In essence, adhere to the principles of Creation by pursuing knowledge and truth, rejecting servitude to individuals or false idols.

Instead, demonstrate empathy and generosity towards those facing hardship, thereby fulfilling the mandate of caring for others in the spirit of universal harmony.

Pursuing the truth

As mentioned in the teachings, what has been brought into existence by the laws of Creation is a manifestation of love conceived within the universal consciousness of the cosmos.

However, many have turned away from this truth, opting instead to believe in gods born from human imagination rather than seeking knowledge and understanding of the fundamental reality.

The path to liberation lies in embracing the truth that offers genuine protection and wisdom.

It requires rejecting false beliefs and illusions that hinder spiritual and intellectual growth.

By confronting these misconceptions and striving for deeper understanding, individuals can transcend the limitations of mere belief and attain true enlightenment.

Therefore, seek clarity and discernment within yourselves.

Embrace the knowledge that leads to liberation from ignorance and falsehoods.

Align your thoughts and actions with the universal truths embedded in the laws of Creation, allowing them to guide you towards genuine spiritual fulfillment and harmony with the cosmos.

Fear or peace

Following these teachings, there exists a profound connection between human beings and the laws of Creation, as well as the laws of nature, which must be respected and honored.

This bond ensures that no fear needs to be harbored towards life or death.

The laws of Creation and natural laws are inherently designed to manifest themselves regardless of circumstances.

However, it is within your power alone to determine whether fear or peace prevails within you based on your adherence to these principles.

By aligning with the laws of Creation and nature, you participate in the natural order of the universe.

This alignment fosters a sense of security and harmony, knowing that life unfolds according to these immutable laws.

Realizing this connection allows you to navigate life's challenges with resilience and confidence, free from unnecessary fear or anxiety.

Conversely, disregarding these laws can lead to discord and uncertainty.

Choosing to act contrary to these principles may disrupt the natural balance, causing turmoil and distress within oneself and the world.

Therefore, by honoring the bond between humanity and the laws of Creation and nature, you contribute to a life filled with clarity, purpose, and serenity.

In essence, recognize and uphold the profound bond between yourself, the laws of Creation, and nature.

Nurture the wisdom inherent in these principles, ensuring that your choices and actions align with the greater harmony of existence. In doing so, you cultivate a life marked by courage, peace, and fulfillment, regardless of the challenges that come your way.

The rewards

People of Earth, contemplate the boundless goodness of life and the benevolent deeds that have been bestowed upon you since time immemorial, meant for all who adhere to the natural and creational laws and principles.

In conformity with these teachings, throughout history, those who have aligned themselves with these inherent laws and guidelines have reaped the benefits of a harmonious existence.

They have experienced the rewards of living in harmony with nature, enjoying its abundance and nurturing its delicate balance.

By respecting these principles, they have found fulfillment and purpose in their lives, contributing positively to their communities and the world at large.

Reflect upon the enduring legacy of those who have walked the path guided by these natural and creational laws.

Their actions have fostered peace, compassion, and unity among humanity, embodying the essence of goodness and righteousness.

Their example inspires others to follow in their footsteps, creating a ripple effect of positivity and transformation.

As you ponder the unceasing generosity of life and the opportunities it presents, consider embracing these laws and guidelines.

Let them guide your actions and decisions, leading you toward a life of meaning, abundance, and fulfillment.

In doing so, you honor the legacy of those who have come before you and pave the way for a future where goodness and harmony prevail for all.

Abundance and fulfillment

According to Billy, the natural laws of Creation embody principles that, when followed and applied, bring about beneficial effects.

Adhering to these laws leads to prosperity, success, joy, love, peace, harmony, and wisdom.

By aligning with these inherent principles, individuals and societies can experience abundance and fulfillment.

These laws promote balance, fairness, and sustainability in all aspects of life.

Nurturing them fosters harmonious relationships, both with oneself and with others, cultivating a sense of unity and interconnectedness.

Furthermore, living in accordance with these natural laws enhances clarity and insight, guiding decisions and actions towards positive outcomes.

They serve as guiding beacons that illuminate pathways toward personal growth, communal well-being, and a harmonious existence with the environment.

In essence, the wisdom inherent in these natural laws offers a framework for living that nurtures holistic prosperity and contributes to a world where happiness, peace, and fulfillment are attainable for all.

The dwellings

Consider this: the dwellings of human beings are the Earths, and they are only temporary abodes.

Therefore, it is imperative to make these dwellings beneficial for fellow humans and for the greater good.

Indeed, according to Billy, refrain from causing harm or destruction to these earthly habitats.

Strive to enhance the environments where people live, ensuring they are sustainable and nurturing.

Learn practices that preserve and protect natural resources, promoting a harmonious coexistence with the Earth and its diverse ecosystems.

Recognize the interconnectedness of all life forms and the responsibility to steward the planet responsibly for future generations.

Let your actions reflect a commitment to sustainability and environmental stewardship. Support initiatives that promote conservation, mitigate climate impact, and uphold the integrity of ecosystems.

By safeguarding the Earth's habitats, you contribute to a healthier and more resilient planet for all inhabitants.

Regard the Earth as a shared home for humanity and endeavor to leave a positive legacy through actions that promote the well-being of people and the planet.

Choose love over animosity

In accordance with the teachings, distance yourselves from those who consider themselves your adversaries.

Yet, let goodness and love guide your actions towards them.

Avoid harboring hatred and instead, remain connected through compassion, even when addressing their wrongful deeds openly.

Never designate someone as your enemy without cause, for your bond with fellow humans is rooted in love and mutual assistance in all virtuous pursuits.

Strive for reconciliation and understanding, even amidst disagreements or perceived hostility.

Accept empathy and seek to bridge divides through dialogue and acts of kindness.

By nurturing a spirit of unity and benevolence, you contribute to the collective well-being of humanity.

Let love and goodwill prevail in your interactions with others, fostering a community where respect and solidarity reign.

Embrace the responsibility to uplift and support one another, ensuring that every action reflects the values of compassion and integrity.

Choose love over animosity and strive to build connections that transcend differences.

Uphold the principle of doing good, even towards those who may oppose you, fostering a world where humanity flourishes through understanding and mutual respect.

Stand firm against evil

As outlined in the teachings, do not deviate from the path of righteousness when confronted with evil.

Refrain from aiding malevolence in any form, lest you face expulsion from your community and endure ostracism for the remainder of your days.

Hold fast to integrity and moral clarity in all your endeavors. Resist the allure of wrongdoing and choose instead to uphold justice, kindness, and compassion.

By standing firm against evil, you safeguard not only your own honor but also contribute to the preservation of peace and harmony within your society.

Be vigilant against the temptations that lead astray.

Remain steadfast in your commitment to principles that uphold dignity and respect for all.

Your actions shape the fabric of your community and define the legacy you leave behind.

Let your choices reflect a steadfast dedication to goodness and truth.

Uphold your responsibilities as stewards of morality and guardians of decency, ensuring that your presence in society remains a beacon of hope and righteousness.

The gifts of nature

As documented in the spiritual teachings, human beings, young and old alike, inhabit the vast garden of Earth, partaking in the abundance bestowed upon them by nature, animals, and their own creations.

Enjoy the fruits of the land and the nourishment derived from animals and other creatures, ensuring gratitude and moderation in all things.

Savor the fermented juices of fruits in measured quantities, avoiding excess that leads to intoxication.

Similarly, consume the flesh of animals—whether birds, fishes, or mammals like pigs, cattle, and camels—but do so conscientiously, without indulging in gluttony or greed that would lead to wrongdoing.

Let the harmony of nature guide your actions, respecting the balance and beauty it offers.

Cherish the sustenance provided by the earth's bounty, mindful of the responsibility to care for it sustainably.

By partaking in food and drink with respect and moderation, you honor the intricate web of life that supports all living beings on this planet.

Strive to cultivate a relationship with the natural world that reflects stewardship and mindfulness.

Embrace the privilege of nourishment from Earth's garden while upholding principles of balance and ethical conduct.

In doing so, you contribute to a world where abundance is shared responsibly, and each individual's actions contribute positively to the collective well-being.

Thus, inhabit Earth's garden with reverence and responsibility, nurturing a harmonious existence that respects the gifts of nature and sustains the delicate balance of life for generations to come.

Past relationship

In every relationship, each person we encounter brings us something valuable—a lesson that holds significance beyond words.

These connections, regardless of their length or intensity, contribute to our growth and understanding in profound ways.

Each relationship, whether fleeting or long-lasting, offers insight that shapes who we become.

When a relationship ends, it can be challenging to let go of feelings like resentment or sadness.

However, there is a strength in choosing gratitude over anger.

Every experience, even the painful ones, teaches us something unique about ourselves and our path.

Embracing this perspective allows us to see past hurts as opportunities for growth rather than burdens to carry.

It is unnecessary to hold onto resentment toward a lost love.

Often, the actions of others—even those that cause us pain—can help us evolve, guiding us closer to inner peace and understanding.

When we accept these experiences as part of our journey, we find a sense of acceptance that transcends individual grievances.

Reaching this inner peace brings us a deeper sense of well-being.

By letting go of negative emotions and cultivating gratitude for the lessons we've learned, we open ourselves up to a richer, more fulfilled life.

This approach allows us to embrace future relationships with wisdom, compassion, and an open heart.

A call to return

As proclaimed by Billy, reflect upon a time when you were free from belief systems that veiled the real truth and were closer to understanding the inherent truths of existence.

It is a call to return to a state where your connection to Creation was rooted not in blind faith or irrational beliefs but in a genuine quest for truth and understanding.

This state of being invites you to rediscover the essence of your connection to the universe, untethered from the confines of organized religion and dogma.

In embracing this return to truth, you reclaim a sense of authenticity in your relationship with Creation.

It entails recognizing the natural order and principles that govern the cosmos, acknowledging the interconnectedness of all life forms and the profound wisdom embedded within the fabric of existence.

By relinquishing dependency on external deities and prayers to gods, you align yourself with a deeper understanding of your role as a conscious participant in the cosmic unfolding.

The journey towards reconnecting with truth involves a process of introspection and discernment. It requires questioning inherited beliefs and societal constructs that may obscure genuine spiritual growth and enlightenment.

By cultivating a direct relationship with Creation based on empirical observation and personal experience, you foster a more profound and meaningful connection to the mysteries of life.

Returning to a state of connection with Creation through truth involves transcending superficial forms of worship or adherence to religious doctrines.

It encourages a reclamation of personal sovereignty and responsibility in navigating the complexities of existence.

By embracing the innate capacity to discern truth from falsehood and to align with universal principles of love, harmony, and compassion, you reclaim agency over your spiritual journey and contribute to a more enlightened and harmonious world.

The call to return to a state of connection with Creation through truth invites human beings to reclaim their innate wisdom and authenticity.

It urges a departure from dogmatic beliefs and organized religion, encouraging a deeper exploration of universal truths and principles that resonate with personal experience and understanding.

By embracing this journey of self-discovery and enlightenment, individuals rediscover their inherent connection to the cosmos and cultivate a more profound sense of purpose and fulfillment in life.

The quest to understand

According to Billy, in the pursuit of truth, you possess the capability to uncover the mysteries concealed within the laws of nature and the principles of Creation.

This proclamation underscores the inherent potential within humanity to delve into the profound truths that govern existence.

By dedicating yourselves to this endeavor, you unlock insights and revelations that have remained obscure due to the limitations imposed by your own imperiousness and preconceptions.

The quest to understand the laws of nature involves a concerted effort to unravel the intricate tapestry of the cosmos.

Through observation, experimentation, and introspection, individuals can discern the underlying patterns and principles that dictate the functioning of the natural world.

This process of exploration not only expands intellectual horizons but also fosters a deeper connection to the environment and a heightened appreciation for the interconnectedness of all living beings.

Similarly, exploring the principles of Creation requires individuals to transcend conventional knowledge and embrace a holistic understanding of existence.

These principles encompass the fundamental forces that shape reality, guiding the evolution of life and consciousness.

By immersing oneself in the study of these principles, individuals gain profound insights into the purpose and interconnectedness that underpin the universe, transcending narrow perspectives and embracing a broader worldview.

The revelation of hidden truths through the study of natural laws and principles of Creation empowers individuals to confront and transcend their own imperiousness—those inherent tendencies towards arrogance or narrow-mindedness.

By humbling oneself before the vastness and complexity of the cosmos, individuals open themselves to transformative experiences and spiritual growth.

This process not only enriches personal understanding but also contributes to the collective wisdom and evolution of humanity as a whole.

The pursuit of truth through the exploration of natural laws and principles of Creation offers humanity a pathway to profound insight and enlightenment.

By overcoming imperiousness and embracing humility, individuals unlock hidden truths that expand their understanding of the universe and their place within it.

Through continuous effort and dedication to unraveling these mysteries, humanity progresses towards a future enriched by knowledge, wisdom, and a deeper connection to the cosmic order.

The sacred bond with truth

When one severs the sacred bond with truth, originally established as a binding force, they unravel the very fabric of peace on Earth.

This bond, according to the teachings, once strong and inviolable, serves as a cornerstone of moral integrity and societal harmony.

However, its dissolution disrupts the delicate balance that sustains collective tranquility. The consequences of such actions are dire, leading not to victory but to inevitable defeat.

Truth, in its essence, acts as a unifying principle that fosters trust, understanding, and mutual respect among individuals and communities.

It transcends mere factual accuracy, embodying honesty, transparency, and ethical conduct.

When this bond is fractured—whether through deceit, falsehoods, or betrayal—it engenders discord and strife.

Such fractures breed mistrust and sow seeds of division, eroding the foundations of societal cohesion.

The ramifications of breaking the bond with truth extend beyond personal repercussions to encompass broader societal implications. Instances of falsehoods and deception undermine the very notion of justice and fairness, leading to an erosion of moral authority and governance.

Societies built on principles of honesty and accountability rely on the integrity of their institutions and individuals.

When these foundations are compromised, the result is a pervasive atmosphere of uncertainty and instability.

At the end, those who disregard or manipulate truth for personal gain or ideological motives ultimately jeopardize their own aspirations for lasting success and fulfillment.

The pursuit of short-term gains through deception and dishonesty may yield temporary advantages, but it ultimately leads to a loss of credibility and trust.

In the grand scheme of human endeavors, genuine progress and prosperity are rooted in a steadfast commitment to truth and integrity.

Only by upholding the sanctity of truth can individuals and societies cultivate enduring peace and collective well-being.

The decision to sever the bond with truth undermines the fundamental pillars of peace and stability on Earth.

It perpetuates cycles of conflict and division, jeopardizing the harmony necessary for societal progress.

The imperative to uphold truth as a binding link is not merely a moral obligation but a practical necessity for fostering trust, resilience, and unity in the face of adversity.

By honoring truth as a sacred commitment, individuals and communities alike can strive toward a future grounded in mutual respect, understanding, and shared prosperity.

Dear Earth people

Dear Earth people, heed the wisdom of those who guide us—the purveyors of truth, the custodians of spiritual enlightenment, and the stewards of life itself.

As stated by Billy, they impart that in the universal order, there exists no beginning or end except for the eternal consciousness that birthed creation and the primal flame from which all emerged and to which all shall return.

Indeed, everything emanates from a singular essence that transcends form and originates from the formless.

These teachings prompt us to contemplate the profound unity underlying all existence—a unity that surpasses the confines of time and space.

They remind us that our essence is intricately interwoven with the fabric of universal consciousness, intimately linked to the primordial flame that sparks the cosmos.

This understanding challenges us to see beyond illusions of separateness, acknowledging the interconnectedness that binds us together.

Embracing this perspective invites profound insights into reality and our place within it.

It encourages exploration into the depths of consciousness and recognition of the eternal cycle of creation and dissolution.

When honoring the unity amidst diversity, we embark on a journey toward spiritual awareness and a harmonious relationship with the cosmos.

Therefore, let us cherish the teachings of these wise mentors—guides who illuminate the path to understanding our origins, purpose, and interconnected destiny within the vast tapestry of existence.

In doing so, we align ourselves with timeless truths that resonate across cultures and eras, guiding humanity toward a future where unity, wisdom, and spiritual enlightenment prevail.

The finality of death

Complying with the creation energy teachings, human life unfolds with the capacity for individuals to shape their existence through creative works, relationships of love, acquisition of knowledge and wisdom, and cultivation of peace, joy, and freedom.

This self-directed evolution aligns with the essence of existence.

However, despite this agency, the timing of death remains beyond human influence.

Even in cases of suicide, where one may attempt to evade death, it only serves to postpone the inevitable moment ordained by mortality.

Thus, suicide ultimately represents a destructive act and a cowardly escape from life's challenges and the responsibility to face both life and death.

Furthermore, the teachings also state that upon death, humans relinquish their physical bodies and all associated earthly strengths.

They also part with cherished family, friends, acquaintances, and all material possessions accumulated throughout their lives.

In the transition to the afterlife, material goods hold no significance, as the realm beyond lacks the physicality of the mortal world.

Departing souls traverse this journey alone, accompanied solely by the energies of spirit and the universal consciousness of creation.

Contemplating mortality reveals a poignant paradox: humans possess the agency to shape their journey on Earth, yet they are inexorably bound by the finality of death.

In death, they must surrender all physical attachments and the comfort of familiar companions, embarking on a solitary journey guided by spiritual essence and the cosmic awareness that transcends mortal boundaries.

After each life

After each life, the personality is erased and reprogrammed for the next incarnation.

The individuality and specific traits from that life do not continue into the next one, as each new life brings a fresh identity.

However, not everything is lost in this process.

What is carried over between lives is the wisdom and knowledge acquired throughout the previous experience.

These insights, gained from the challenges and lessons of past lives, are preserved for future growth and development, though not consciously remembered.

This accumulated wisdom and knowledge are stored in the subconscious mind.

While the new personality in the next life may not have direct access to past memories, the deeper understanding remains, silently influencing decisions and perspectives.

The next personality can access this knowledge if they practice the right concentration techniques.

Through focused meditation or mental discipline, the new self can unlock the wisdom stored in the subconscious and benefit from the lessons learned in past lives.

Born of ignorance

In accordance with the creation energy teachings, the beauty inherent in all things and the unmistakable signs of Creation's origins and nature are designed to captivate you, revealing the truth and grace embedded within Creation's laws and guidance.

Despite this, there are many among you who dismiss the true essence and those who possess profound knowledge of it.

Nevertheless, Creation itself, alongside prophets and those enlightened with truth, stands by you with love, freedom, peace, and harmony, extending their grace.

They understand that in your ignorance, you unwittingly commit actions that defy Creation, truth, knowledgeable individuals, and truth proclaimers.

The teachings continue to say your lack of awareness blinds you to the repercussions of your actions against Creation and those who uphold the truth.

However, this ignorance and the consequent misguided behavior are seen with forgiveness, as you have been misled and must undergo a learning process.

The manifestations of beauty in the world and the undeniable signs of Creation are intended to draw you closer to understanding its essence and purpose.

Yet, the rejection of these truths by some individuals does not diminish the support and compassion extended to all.

Creation and its emissaries offer love, freedom, peace, and harmony, embracing humanity despite its errors born of ignorance.

In the journey towards enlightenment, the teachings say forgiveness is extended to those who act unknowingly against the principles of Creation and truth.

The path to understanding is fraught with challenges, but through learning and growth, individuals can overcome their ignorance and align themselves with the profound truths and principles that govern existence.

The cycle of disappointment

In accordance with the teachings, when you align your actions accordingly, you will also find earthly gains abundant.

This is because you leverage the advantage of expecting only what space, time, and your fellow human beings genuinely offer.

This perspective ensures you are never disappointed and enables you to live in love, peace, freedom, and harmony with yourself, others, and your environment.

By adopting this approach, you cultivate a mindset of gratitude and acceptance.

You appreciate the gifts and opportunities presented by each moment and relationship without imposing unrealistic expectations.

This pragmatic outlook fosters contentment and fulfillment as you focus on making the most of what life offers in its true essence.

The teachings tell us that living in alignment with reality allows you to build genuine connections with others based on mutual respect and understanding.

It promotes harmonious relationships where compassion and empathy thrive, creating a supportive environment for personal growth and collective well-being.

Moreover, this approach liberates you from the cycle of disappointment and dissatisfaction that often accompanies unrealistic expectations.

Instead, you embrace life with an open heart and a clear mind, navigating challenges with resilience and grace.

Therefore, by embracing the reality of what is achievable and valuable in each moment, you unlock the potential for profound happiness and fulfillment.

This mindful approach not only enriches your own life but also contributes positively to the harmony and balance of the world around you.

Alignment and harmony

What is essential is not to indulge in mere rumination but to consciously engage with your thoughts, feelings, intellect, and rationality.

Through this conscious engagement, you embark on a journey to uncover the inherent truth within yourselves—the ultimate truth and culmination point.

This pursuit leads you to discover the truth of all truths embedded within the Universal Consciousness of Creation and its governing laws and recommendations.

According to the teachings, by abandoning incessant rumination and embracing this path, you cultivate within yourself a state characterized by true love, joy, peace, freedom, and harmony.

These states are not arbitrary; they are inherently structured by the effects of Creation's laws and recommendations.

This transformation occurs as you align your thoughts, emotions, and actions with these universal principles.

To achieve this state of alignment and harmony, it is crucial to move beyond passive reflection and into active exploration and application of spiritual truths.

Rather than dwelling on past concerns or hypothetical scenarios, you focus on understanding and living in accordance with the laws of Creation.

This proactive approach fosters personal growth and contributes positively to the collective consciousness.

In essence, the path to true fulfillment lies in utilizing your faculties—thoughts, feelings, intellect, and rationality—with conscious intent and purpose.

By doing so, you uncover the profound truths that govern existence and align yourself with the harmonious principles of Creation.

This journey not only enriches your individual experience but also contributes to the greater harmony and balance of the universe as a whole.

Striving to perceive

Following the teachings, if you desire to avoid stagnation on a single developmental step for a significant portion of your life and wish to prevent recurrent setbacks, it is essential to exert significant effort in perceiving the entirety of the present moment.

This means understanding the material aspects, delving into your inner self, and exploring the subtle energies that permeate existence.

By comprehending these dimensions with clarity, experiencing them fully, and integrating them into your life, you can elevate your understanding to wisdom.

Achieving this holistic awareness and integration allows you to derive evolutionary and consciousness-based benefits.

It involves actively engaging with the challenges and opportunities presented by each moment and embracing them as avenues for growth.

Through this process, you not only accumulate knowledge and experience but also deepen your connection to your higher self and the broader spiritual essence of existence.

The pursuit of wisdom through comprehensive living requires dedication and mindfulness.

It demands a commitment to self-reflection, learning from every experience, and cultivating resilience in the face of adversity.

By consistently striving to perceive, understand, and integrate the full spectrum of existence—both tangible and intangible—you empower yourself to transcend limitations and evolve towards higher states of consciousness and fulfillment.

In essence, the path to continuous growth and advancement lies in embracing the richness of each present moment.

By making deliberate efforts to engage deeply with all aspects of your being and environment, you pave the way for profound personal transformation and spiritual evolution.

This approach not only enriches your own life journey but also contributes positively to the collective consciousness of humanity.

The transformative potential

Pursuing the teachings, the evolutionary steps that individuals must construct and utilize for their ascent should not be approached hastily.

Superficially developed steps risk collapsing when attempting to progress to the next level.

However, there exists a natural safeguard against this risk during the ascent: each higher developmental stage can only be attained through the complete development and integration of the current step.

This principle emphasizes the importance of thoroughness and mindfulness in each phase of personal growth.

Rushing through or neglecting the foundational aspects of a developmental stage can undermine its stability and hinder progress.

Instead, by fully immersing oneself in the challenges and lessons of the present stage, individuals lay a solid foundation for the subsequent evolutionary leap.

The process of climbing to higher levels of consciousness and personal evolution demands patience, dedication, and a willingness to engage deeply with one's experiences.

It requires embracing the transformative potential inherent in each developmental phase and integrating its lessons into one's life with authenticity and commitment.

By honoring the integrity of each step and allowing its natural unfolding, individuals not only fortify their spiritual and personal growth but also ensure a sustainable progression towards higher states of awareness and fulfillment.

This approach fosters resilience and depth, enabling individuals to navigate challenges effectively and evolve harmoniously along their evolutionary journey.

Honing spiritual practices

In accordance with the teachings, the key focus lies in nurturing the high fulfillment of your consciousness evolution and diligently attending to the individual development steps necessary for your spiritual growth.

These steps are essential constructs that you must actively build and integrate into your life in order to achieve fulfillment and progress along your evolutionary path.

Central to this journey is the cultivation of awareness and mindfulness in every aspect of existence.

By conscientiously engaging with each developmental phase and learning from the experiences it offers, you enhance your understanding and wisdom.

This process involves embracing challenges as opportunities for growth, honing spiritual practices, and deepening introspection.

Your evolution unfolds through the deliberate application of spiritual principles and the continuous refinement of your consciousness.

This requires not only personal development but also contributing positively to the collective consciousness of humanity.

Each step forward in your evolution serves to elevate not only your own spiritual awareness but also the interconnected web of existence.

The pursuit of high-consciousness fulfillment requires dedication, perseverance, and a commitment to inner transformation.

By nurturing your individual development steps with sincerity and diligence, you empower yourself to transcend limitations, expand consciousness, and align with the higher purpose of your evolution.

Self-discovery and transformation

In conformity with the teachings, the consciousness evolution continues throughout your entire current lifetime, just as it has unfolded in all your previous lives as different personalities.

It will also persist in future lives, where you will inhabit new identities after leaving your current existence.

Each life represents a unique chapter in an ongoing journey of growth and development.

Through successive incarnations, you accumulate experiences, learn lessons, and undergo personal evolution.

The cycle of life and rebirth offers opportunities to explore different facets of existence, refine understanding, and advance spiritually.

The continuity of this process across lifetimes underscores the interconnectedness of your soul's journey through time and space.

Each incarnation builds upon the lessons and achievements of previous ones, contributing to the broader tapestry of your spiritual evolution.

As you transition from one life to the next, you carry forward the wisdom and karmic imprints accumulated over lifetimes.

This ongoing journey of self-discovery and transformation is guided by the principle of growth through experience, shaping your understanding and approach to life in each subsequent incarnation.

Embracing this perspective invites a deeper appreciation for the interconnectedness of life's experiences and the cyclical nature of spiritual evolution.

It encourages a mindful approach to living, where each moment and interaction contributes to the unfolding narrative of your soul's journey across multiple lifetimes.

Facial appearance

As stated in the teachings, indeed, observing human faces can reveal detailed life stories to those who are perceptive and knowledgeable in this area.

As individuals age, their faces increasingly reflect their practical experiences and the cumulative impact of their lives.

The variations in impulsations and processing of feelings, psyche, emotions, and thoughts are all recorded on the face, allowing experts in physiognomy to interpret these expressions like a book.

This ability to read life stories through facial features is not limited to older individuals.

Even young people exhibit a range of facial features and physiognomic characteristics that provide insights into their life experiences, morality, and character.

Faces reveal more than just wrinkles; they display a variety of distinct traits that reflect the individual's life and lifestyle.

In essence, the features and expressions on a face serve as a record of one's inner life and experiences.

Skilled observers can discern much about a person's character and experiences through their facial appearance.

Overall, faces offer a rich tapestry of information about individuals, providing clues about their life stories, characters, and experiences, regardless of their age.

Holistic perspective

The teachings stated If one does not fully engage in the developmental process by actively experiencing and living in the present moment—both in the physical realm and within their inner and subtle energetic dimensions—then they cannot mature or progress to the next stage of development.

It is through genuine and immersive engagement across all facets of existence—spiritual, emotional, mental, and physical—that individuals generate the necessary energy and insight to perceive and ascend to the next developmental level.

True growth and evolution require more than passive observation or theoretical understanding; they demand active participation and integration of experiences into one's daily life.

By embracing and fully living in the present moment, individuals harness the transformative power inherent in each experience.

This involves not only engaging with the material aspects of life but also exploring the depths of their inner being and the subtle energies that permeate existence.

The integration of experiences across these domains—inner, fine-fluidal (subtle energies), and material—serves as a catalyst for personal growth and spiritual advancement.

It cultivates a holistic perspective that enables individuals to perceive and align with their next developmental step.

This process generates the energy and clarity needed to navigate challenges, expand consciousness, and evolve toward higher states of awareness and fulfillment.

Eventually, the journey towards higher development unfolds through active participation in life's experiences, both tangible and intangible.

By nurturing the present moment and engaging fully with all dimensions of existence, individuals empower themselves to recognize, embrace, and ascend to the next stage of their evolutionary path.

Transformative lessons

In keeping with the teachings, the progression to higher developmental stages hinges solely upon the complete and absolute fulfillment of each preceding step.

This entails perceiving, comprehending, knowing, practically experiencing, and fully integrating each developmental phase into one's present life.

Without achieving this comprehensive understanding and living out of each step, one cannot grasp the essence of the whole—a wisdom that forms the foundation of the advanced developmental state attained.

Each developmental phase offers unique lessons and insights that must be fully embraced and embodied. It is through active engagement and practical application that individuals acquire profound wisdom.

This wisdom transcends mere theoretical knowledge; it encompasses deep understanding gained through personal experience and reflection.

The process of climbing to higher developmental stages demands a commitment to continuous learning and growth.

It requires individuals to immerse themselves fully in the challenges and lessons presented by each stage, thereby internalizing the wisdom embedded within.

This transformative journey involves not only acquiring knowledge but also embodying the principles and values that facilitate spiritual, emotional, and intellectual evolution.

By honoring the importance of each developmental step and diligently pursuing holistic growth, individuals can cultivate the wisdom necessary to navigate complex challenges and achieve higher states of consciousness and fulfillment.

This journey of self-discovery and enlightenment unfolds through the sincere dedication to learning, integrating, and embodying the transformative lessons of each developmental phase.

Mindfulness and ethical integrity

According to the teachings, understand that your self-created destiny unfailingly aligns with the meticulous nuances of justice and corresponds precisely to the effects governed by creational laws.

Through the magnetic attraction and accumulation of your own thoughts, feelings, deeds, actions, and overall activity, you continuously draw similar energies toward yourself.

These energies inevitably return to you, strengthened and exact in accordance with the causes you originally set in motion, irrespective of whether they were directed towards yourself, loved ones, or humanity at large.

This process remains consistent and unwavering: what you emit into the universe through your thoughts and actions is mirrored back to you in kind.

The dynamics of cause and effect dictate that every intention and action carries inherent consequences that echo through the fabric of existence.

This cosmic law operates with precision, ensuring that the outcomes you experience are intricately woven into the fabric of your personal journey.

The fairness and precision of this process lie in its adherence to universal principles of balance and reciprocity.

It underscores the importance of mindfulness and ethical integrity in every decision and interaction.

By recognizing this inherent law of cause and effect, individuals can harness their creative power responsibly, knowing that their choices shape not only their immediate circumstances but also the overarching trajectory of their lives.

At the end, this understanding invites individuals to take ownership of their destinies with clarity and purpose.

By aligning thoughts, emotions, and actions with positive intentions and harmonious principles, individuals can cultivate a reality that resonates with joy, fulfillment, and meaningful connection.

Realizing this awareness empowers individuals to navigate life's challenges with resilience and wisdom, contributing to their personal growth and the collective evolution of humanity.

Ownership of thoughts

Following the teachings, through the accumulation of energy and power stemming from thought and feeling-based causes, a process of increasing density unfolds.

This compaction eventually manifests as a tangible, substantial factor— what we perceive as destiny.

This destiny is the culmination that the creator of the original thoughts and feelings must inevitably face, live through, and resolve on their own.

This process elucidates the true nature of destiny, often feared and misunderstood, as an effect stemming directly from causes that individuals themselves have generated.

The development of destiny unfolds as a natural consequence of the energetic forces set in motion by human thoughts and emotions.

As these energies accumulate and intensify, they coalesce into a palpable reality that individuals must confront and navigate.

This process is not arbitrary or externally imposed but rather emerges as a direct result of the intentions, attitudes, and actions individuals choose to embody and express.

Understanding this developmental process of destiny underscores the profound influence individuals wield over their own lives.

It emphasizes the importance of conscious awareness and responsible decision-making in shaping personal outcomes and trajectories.

Each thought, feeling, and action contributes to the ongoing evolution of one's destiny, highlighting the interconnectedness between cause and effect in the fabric of existence.

The journey through one's destiny represents an opportunity for growth, learning, and self-realization.

By embracing the consequences of their own creations, individuals can engage in a process of self-discovery and transformation.

This perspective encourages individuals to take ownership of their thoughts and emotions, recognizing their power to shape not only personal destinies but also contribute to the collective evolution of humanity as a whole.

Cycles of discord

Pursuant to the teachings, the law of interaction and, consequently, your destiny, the humanity of Earth, operates on the principle of attracting similar energies through the motion of creation—be it thoughts, emotions, actions, or any form of activity.

This attraction creates a symbiotic connection where similar energies reinforce each other, leading to the formation of a powerful energy source.

This accumulation of energy becomes a significant force with tremendous power, acting as a transmitter that reciprocates and returns everything back to its origin.

This dynamic process underscores the interconnectedness of all actions and intentions.

When individuals generate thoughts, emotions, or actions of a particular quality, they attract corresponding energies from their environment and beyond.

This mutual attraction forms a feedback loop where energies resonate and amplify, contributing to the creation of a potent energetic field.

The culmination of these interactions results in a collective energy reservoir that exerts influence over personal and collective destinies.

This energy field functions not only as a receiver but also as a sender, emitting vibrations and influences that reverberate through the interconnected web of human consciousness and beyond.

Understanding this principle invites individuals to be mindful of the energies they emit and attract.

By cultivating positive thoughts, emotions, and actions, individuals contribute to the harmonious evolution of their own destinies and the collective destiny of humanity.

Conversely, negative or destructive energies perpetuate cycles of discord and adversity, affecting both immediate outcomes and long-term trajectories.

The law of interaction and destiny highlights the profound impact of human intention and action on the unfolding tapestry of existence.

It underscores the responsibility each individual bears in shaping not only their personal reality but also the broader collective experience through conscious and intentional living.

Misconception

Many Earth humans hold a grave misconception that life should be free of challenges.

They fail to recognize that material life is meant to be a classroom filled with problems to solve that are necessary for their growth and improvement.

These challenges are not meant to be avoided but embraced as opportunities to develop and evolve.

Unfortunately, because of widespread ignorance, when faced with difficulties, Earth humans often respond by seeking divine intervention rather than taking practical steps to address the situation.

They look outward for help from deities that do not exist, believing that prayer alone can resolve their struggles.

This reliance on external forces prevents them from engaging with the lessons each challenge offers.

Instead of learning to navigate life's complexities and growing through problem-solving, they become passive participants in their own existence.

This hinders their progress and robs them of important life experiences.

By turning away from self-reliance and critical thinking, Earth humans miss out on the very lessons that would enhance their lives.

Their refusal to face challenges head-on keeps them trapped in a cycle of ignorance, limiting their potential for personal growth and evolution.

Shaping personal destiny

According to the teachings, as the creator of your decisions and volition, you are fundamentally linked to the causes you set in motion.

This connection ensures that everything, whether perceived as destiny or interaction, continually returns to influence you.

This principle holds true regardless of the timeframe—whether consequences manifest swiftly or after considerable time has passed—and regardless of whether the initial cause was benevolent or malevolent in nature.

Every decision made, whether consciously or unconsciously, carries the potential to shape future outcomes and affect personal destiny.

This interconnectedness means that actions taken today may reverberate back to impact your life, sometimes unexpectedly, in the future.

This concept transcends the distinction between good and evil; it encompasses all choices and their subsequent repercussions.

The notion of causality underscores the accountability individuals bear for their decisions.

It emphasizes the importance of mindful consideration and ethical awareness in decision-making processes.

By recognizing this interconnected web of causation, individuals can take responsibility for their actions and strive to align their choices with principles that promote harmony and well-being for themselves and others.

The continuity of cause and effect in human experience reflects a universal truth: every action carries consequences that ultimately circle back to affect the individual who initiated them.

This understanding invites reflection on the ethical dimensions of decision-making and encourages a proactive approach to shaping personal destiny through conscious and deliberate choices.

The power to defend against attacks

The psychological and consciousness states of individuals—whether it be oneself, loved ones, or fellow human beings—always play a crucial role.

This means that no one is defenseless against attacks, whether these attacks originate internally or externally.

Each person has the capacity to defend themselves and others against negative influences, whether they arise from within their own psyche or from external sources.

Indeed, according to the teachings, self-defense against harmful thoughts and emotions begins with cultivating awareness and inner strength.

By developing a deep understanding of one's own psychological vulnerabilities and strengths, individuals can fortify themselves against the detrimental effects of negativity.

This includes practicing mindfulness, cultivating positive thinking patterns, and seeking support from others when needed.

Similarly, individuals can defend themselves and others against external attacks by fostering supportive relationships and communities.

When individuals come together to promote empathy, understanding, and mutual respect, they create a collective shield against harmful energies and intentions.

This collective defense mechanism is strengthened through communication, compassion, and solidarity among all members of society.

Furthermore, the ability to defend oneself extends beyond mere physical protection to include emotional and spiritual resilience.

By nurturing a resilient mindset and fostering healthy coping mechanisms, individuals can mitigate the impact of negative influences on their mental and emotional well-being.

Finally, the power to defend against attacks—whether they originate internally or externally—lies within the realm of individual and collective consciousness.

By acknowledging and harnessing this power, individuals can create a more supportive and protective environment for themselves, their loved ones, and their communities.

Cultivating inner strength

The teachings show the impact of evil and terrible thoughts and feelings on oneself, others, or humanity hinges entirely upon the psychological and conscious states of the individuals involved.

It is within these inner realms that the potential for harm manifests and takes effect.

The ability of such negativity to inflict harm is not solely determined by its outward expression or physical actions but is profoundly influenced by the receptive state of consciousness and psychic condition of those affected.

Individuals who are emotionally and spiritually resilient may be less susceptible to the harmful effects of negative thoughts and feelings directed toward them.

Conversely, those who are vulnerable or psychologically fragile may experience greater harm from such attacks, even if they are not overtly expressed through physical actions.

The interplay between the sender and the receiver in this context is crucial.

The sender's intent and the receiver's openness or susceptibility together determine the extent to which harmful energies can penetrate and cause disruption.

This dynamic underscores the importance of cultivating inner strength, resilience, and a positive mindset as defenses against psychic and emotional harm.

Moreover, the nature of the harm inflicted can vary widely based on these factors. It may manifest as emotional distress, psychological turmoil, interpersonal conflict, or even physical illness in extreme cases.

The complexity of human consciousness means that the effects of negative thoughts and feelings are not always immediately visible but can unfold over time, influencing relationships, well-being, and overall quality of life.

In essence, the psychic and consciousness-based conditions of individuals play a pivotal role in shaping how harmful thoughts and feelings impact themselves, others, and humanity at large.

Awareness of this dynamic underscores the importance of cultivating empathy, compassion, and positivity in our interactions, fostering a healthier and more harmonious collective existence.

Like attracts like

The teachings state when one chooses to entertain thoughts or commit actions that are harmful or malevolent towards oneself, others, or humanity as a whole, they initiate a chain of consequences that extends beyond immediate perception.

Whether these actions manifest in thoughts, emotions, deeds, or words, they unleash a force into the world that perpetuates itself according to its nature.

This force operates independently of whether its effects are immediately observable in the physical realm or remain concealed in the realms of energy and intention.

The impact of such decisions transcends the visible and tangible, extending into realms that are subtle and ethereal.

This includes the realms of fine energy and fluid dynamics, as well as more substantial and concrete manifestations.

The repercussions of these choices ripple through existence, influencing both the individual who initiated them and the broader fabric of society.

Each decision to engage in negativity or harm contributes to the creation of a cycle where such energies gain momentum and perpetuate themselves.

This cycle operates on the principle that like attracts like, drawing similar energies and intentions into its sphere of influence.

Thus, the initial decision to entertain harmful thoughts or perpetrate hurtful actions sets in motion a dynamic that continues to exert influence and shape outcomes over time.

Ultimately, the significance of our choices lies not only in their immediate consequences but also in the enduring ripple effects they generate.

By recognizing the interconnected nature of our actions and their broader impact, we can strive to cultivate positivity, compassion, and understanding in our interactions with ourselves and others.

This awareness serves as a guiding principle in navigating the complexities of personal and collective existence.

Modesty

According to the teachings, modesty epitomizes the genuine nature of those among your kind who navigate life with integrity and fairness, aligning their words and actions accordingly.

Trust, essential in human relationships, cannot be placed in those who seek to elevate themselves above others.

True trust is bestowed upon individuals who embrace modesty in both their personal conduct and interactions with others.

The essence of modesty lies in humility and sincerity, qualities that cultivate trust and respect among peers.

Those who embody modesty refrain from boasting or seeking undue attention, opting instead to lead by example through their actions and ethical choices.

By adhering to principles of honesty and fairness, they earn the confidence and reliance of those around them.

In contrast, individuals who strive to elevate themselves often undermine trust and credibility.

Their actions, motivated by ego and a desire for recognition, create barriers to genuine connection and mutual respect.

Trust is fragile and easily eroded when sincerity and modesty are overshadowed by self-promotion and arrogance.

The foundation of trust rests upon the consistent demonstration of modesty in both words and deeds.

Those who practice modesty not only uphold the integrity of their character but also foster harmonious relationships built on mutual respect and authenticity.

In nurturing humility and fairness, individuals cultivate an environment where trust can thrive, enriching their interactions and contributing positively to the collective well-being of their community.

Fraught with turmoil

Pursuant to the teachings, it's said that many among us revel in megalomania and selfishness, striving to bask in the spotlight of your peers and gain their admiration.

This pursuit often originates from a corrupted nature and a troubled psyche, driven by a deep-seated desire to outshine others.

However, these efforts are steeped in immodesty and a relentless quest for personal validation, leading to an existence devoid of true joy and fairness.

Your happiness becomes as fragile as decaying wood, and your actions are akin to the futile decay of rotting fruit.

The fixation on self-promotion and the allure of public attention can distort your true nature and inner peace.

By placing undue emphasis on outward appearances and the perceptions of others, you risk losing sight of genuine fulfillment and lasting contentment.

The relentless pursuit of recognition leaves many spiritually bankrupt, as the pursuit of superficial achievements fails to nourish deeper emotional needs.

In this pursuit, there lies a fundamental contradiction: while you strive to project an image of happiness and success, your inner world often remains fraught with turmoil and dissatisfaction.

The fleeting nature of your happiness mirrors the fragile state of decaying wood, susceptible to collapse under the weight of reality.

Your actions, driven by selfish desires and a craving for validation, bear little fruit of lasting value, resembling the insignificance of decaying and rotting fruit.

After all, the path of self-centeredness and vanity proves unsustainable, offering only a fleeting facade of happiness and fulfillment.

The pursuit of superficial acclaim and attention, rooted in ego and self-interest, masks a deeper yearning for genuine connection and purpose.

Until this inner conflict is resolved, you risk perpetuating a cycle of dissatisfaction and spiritual emptiness, your life paralleling the transient existence of decaying wood and rotting fruit.

Live and let live

Following the teachings, human actions should not consume your thoughts excessively.

If you offer guidance and it is rejected, it is best to accept this and move forward.

Assistance should only be extended to those who actively seek it. "Live and let live" ought to be the guiding principle for all individuals, fostering inner peace as a result.

It is important not to dwell overly on the actions of others.

If you attempt to offer advice or insight and encounter resistance, it is wise to respect their choice and focus on your own path.

Helping others is most effective when they are receptive to it.

This approach fosters a harmonious existence where each person's autonomy is respected.

"Live and let live" encapsulates the philosophy of allowing others the freedom to live their lives as they choose, without undue interference.

Welcoming this mindset promotes a tranquil inner state, emphasizing acceptance and understanding.

It encourages individuals to prioritize their own growth and well-being while respecting the autonomy of those around them.

Inner peace is found in accepting that you can only control your own actions and responses.

By focusing on your journey and offering support to those who actively seek it, you contribute positively to your own well-being and that of others.

This approach cultivates a community where mutual respect and personal growth flourish, guided by the simple yet profound principle of "live and let live."

Embracing our flows

Each person must turn inward to understand their true position rather than chasing an unattainable ideal.

By staying grounded in the present truths rather than dreams of perfection, we come to see that perfection is a mere illusion.

We learn and grow from our missteps, with each stumble revealing new lessons and opportunities for personal development.

Our shared imperfections bind us together, creating a tapestry of collective experiences.

No one's journey is superior to another's; through our interconnected paths, we discover our collective resilience and strength.

This mutual journey underscores the importance of recognizing that everyone's experiences contribute to our shared human story.

Embracing each lesson from our mistakes is crucial, as true wisdom often emerges from these moments.

Accepting ourselves with all our flaws allows us to cultivate compassion and grace, enriching our human interactions and personal growth.

By fully accepting ourselves, imperfections and all, we foster deeper connections and a more meaningful existence.

This acceptance nurtures a compassionate and understanding outlook, enhancing both our individual lives and our collective life experience.

The confines of rumination

The teachings tell us it is imperative to choose the path that leads to enlightenment and evolution of consciousness, steering clear of the detrimental path of rumination.

Rumination does not guide toward truth and spiritual growth but rather descends into ignorance, falsehoods, and irresponsibility.

Engaging in endless rumination binds individuals in a cycle where they circle around their own thoughts without achieving true fulfillment.

Rumination often leads individuals to focus selectively on aspects of themselves that are pleasing or comforting, thereby limiting their capacity for deeper self-awareness and growth.

This narrow perspective inhibits the pursuit of higher levels of consciousness and spiritual fulfillment.

To progress along the right path, it is essential to transcend the confines of rumination by actively seeking truth and embracing personal responsibility.

This involves broadening one's perspective beyond self-centered thoughts and embracing a holistic view that aligns with universal principles and laws.

By abandoning the fruitless cycle of rumination and embracing a path of conscious growth and awareness, individuals can aspire to achieve greater fulfillment in their journey of spiritual evolution.

This shift enables them to contribute positively to their own development and to the collective consciousness, fostering harmony and enlightenment in the world around them.

With you alone

The reality is that contemporary humans on Earth have lost an understanding of what consciousness truly is.

Misguided by incorrect teachings from various prophets, religions, ideologies, and philosophies, you have mistakenly attributed the source of your ideas, thoughts, feelings, and actions to the spirit or spirit form.

This misattribution has led to a fundamental misunderstanding of the true nature of consciousness.

According to the teachings, in truth, it is not the spirit or spirit form that governs these aspects of your mental and emotional life.

Instead, it is your consciousness that is responsible for your intellectual activities, thoughts, and actions.

The spirit is not the origin of your mental processes; rather, consciousness plays the central role.

You are fully accountable for the workings of your consciousness, including the resulting intellect and rationality.

This responsibility lies with you alone, as consciousness is the true source of your mental functions and personal actions.

Therefore, it is essential to correct this misconception and recognize that consciousness, not the spirit, is the primary driver of your thoughts and behaviors.

Understanding this distinction is crucial for taking full responsibility for your mental and intellectual development.

As the Herald stated

As indicated in the Creation Energy Teachings, when a person truly grasps the power of their own thoughts, they embed this truth deeply into their subconscious.

Recognizing the profound impact that thoughts can have leads to gradual but significant positive changes in life.

This understanding helps individuals cease actions they previously engaged in without clear reasons, allowing them to align more closely with their true desires and preferences.

As this awareness grows, people begin to focus on activities that bring them joy and fulfillment.

They discover a deeper sense of purpose in their lives, realizing that their own well-being contributes to creating a better world for all living beings and the planet itself.

This insight becomes a driving force in their lives, leading them to embrace personal responsibility and extend that responsibility to the broader environment and its inhabitants.

Those who fully embrace this understanding experience a heightened sense of happiness and satisfaction.

They become committed to managing their lives responsibly and sharing their newfound wisdom with others.

This commitment transcends individual differences, including gender, age, education, wealth, and social status, as the principles underlying this truth are universally applicable.

As the Herald said, the joy of sharing such transformative knowledge is universal.

It unites people from all walks of life, regardless of their background or circumstances, demonstrating that these principles are fundamental and relevant to every human being.

343

If we are able to procreate together, then we are the same race.

It's ignorance that divides us.

At the beginning of time, creation produced 7x7x7, or 343, different skin colors for humanoids.

The idea that one color is superior to another is nothing more than pure ignorance, a misunderstanding of the beauty inherent in diversity.

Imagine living in a world where every rose was white.

It would feel monotonous, wouldn't it?

The beauty of nature lies in its variety, in the countless colors and forms that make up the whole.

In the same way, human beings with their many skin tones represent the intentional diversity of creation, adding richness and depth to life.

Creation, in its infinite brilliance, knows no bounds.

It continuously brings forth a vast array of colors, shapes, and forms, each one as beautiful as the next.

Just as no single flower is more valuable than another, all human skin colors are equally beautiful and worthy of respect.

In recognizing the equal beauty of all colors, we come to see the inherent equality in all human beings.

Creation does not play favorites.

It embraces diversity as part of its design.

If we can see the world through this lens, we will understand that our differences are what make us stronger, not what should tear us apart.

A Compass

Be assured that your destiny is not controlled by external powers, whether they are gods or false idols.

The ultimate authority lies in the all-mightiness of Creation, which manifests through its laws and guidance.

These laws are meant to be followed willingly, guiding individuals toward a path of righteousness and moral integrity.

In adherence to the teachings, the laws of Creation do not impose mandates or dictate fate; instead, they respect and uphold the freedom of individual will.

This freedom allows each person to make choices and decisions autonomously, without external imposition or coercion.

It is a principle that honors personal responsibility and encourages thoughtful consideration in actions and behaviors.

By following the laws and guidance of Creation, individuals embrace a framework that promotes ethical conduct, justice, and harmony.

They are empowered to act with integrity and moral clarity, contributing positively to their own growth and the well-being of others.

This adherence to universal principles fosters a sense of accountability and purpose in navigating life's challenges.

Undoubtedly, the laws and guidance of Creation serve as a compass for individuals seeking to align their lives with truth and virtue.

They provide a foundation for personal development and societal harmony, ensuring that choices are made conscientiously and in alignment with universal values.

This freedom to choose is a cornerstone of human dignity and autonomy, enabling individuals to chart their own course while respecting the rights and freedoms of others.

Observation and consideration

As the teachings stated, during walks and moments of rest, it is crucial to attentively hear, observe, and consider everything in the environment.

Flowers, animals, trees, birds, and every sound and sight encountered hold significant value.

Each detail, no matter how small, contributes to a deeper understanding of the surroundings.

The emphasis on accurate observation and consideration implies that one should engage with the environment on a profound level rather than merely skimming the surface.

It is essential to fully perceive and reflect upon every detail to capture the essence of the experience genuinely.

Such careful attention and reflection lead to neutral and positive thoughts.

These thoughts, in turn, become deeply embedded in memory, forming lasting impressions that enhance recollection and concentration.

This process strengthens mental faculties and deepens the connection with one's experiences.

By dedicating oneself to thorough observation and consideration, the richness of the environment is fully appreciated.

This practice not only enriches personal experiences but also reinforces cognitive abilities and memory retention.

The concept of Hell

The concept of hell as a place of eternal suffering fundamentally conflicts with the nature of the Spirit form or Creation Energy within human beings.

This Spirit is considered to be an eternal, immaterial essence that cannot be harmed by physical elements like fire.

Given that this Spirit form is seen as invulnerable and unchangeable, the idea that hell could inflict any form of suffering upon it is inherently contradictory.

If this essence is indeed as described in the Creation Energy Teachings, it would be unaffected by any external torment.

Moreover, if we accept that the Spirit form is an aspect of Creation Energy, then the notion of hell would be inconsistent with the intrinsic nature of this divine essence.

The Spirit, by its very definition, is meant to be eternal and beyond the reach of material conditions.

To propose that it could be subject to suffering or destruction by fire or any other means undermines the invulnerability of the Spirit form.

In rejecting the idea of hell based on the nature of the Spirit form, we challenge traditional religious and spiritual views.

This rejection shifts our understanding of divine justice and the nature of suffering, questioning established doctrines about the afterlife.

Doing so provokes a re-evaluation of moral and theological beliefs that have long been considered foundational.

Truly, this perspective represents a significant departure from conventional religious thought.

It calls into question the existence of hell and suggests that such a concept is incompatible with the idea of an eternal, invulnerable Spirit form.

This shift prompts a broader reconsideration of how we understand divinity, morality, and the nature of existence itself.

Faith

Faith acts as the driving force within the believer, shaping and molding their character while simultaneously fostering internal darkness.

It operates as a powerful influence, creating both the strengths and the flaws within them. T

As the teachings stated, the believer's own sense of faith becomes a tool for their desires and actions, but it is ultimately based on illusions and misconceptions.

This faith, while seemingly a source of strength, deceives the believer with false promises of joy and fulfillment.

Instead of offering genuine happiness, it leads to misguided hope and eventual suffering.

The believer is ensnared by this deceptive belief, which promises more than it can deliver and thus exacerbates their internal strife.

By adhering to their faith, the believer breaks through the natural bounds of life, only to find that their existence becomes a mere reflection of their own misguided thoughts.

Their perception of reality is distorted by their beliefs, leading to a life that is shaped more by their internal illusions than by any external truths.

The believer's life becomes a mirror image of their own illusory thinking.

The nature of their existence is dictated by the delusions they harbor, resulting in a life characterized more by the distortions of their faith than by any authentic experience or understanding.

Glass house

A significant issue among Earth people today is their tendency to see themselves as the ultimate arbiters of behavior and morality.

Many individuals act as though it is their role to dictate how others should live, offering criticism and judgment on various aspects of others' lives.

This self-assumed authority often leads to a pervasive sense of moral superiority and control.

However, this inclination to oversee and critique others is often accompanied by a failure to assess one's own situation critically.

While people may focus on correcting or criticizing others, they frequently overlook their own flaws and personal issues.

This lack of self-awareness undermines their ability to engage in meaningful self-improvement.

The irony here is that those who assume the role of critics are often themselves like sheep, following societal norms without question and failing to address their own shortcomings.

Their focus on controlling and judging others reflects a deeper issue of personal insecurity and a reluctance to confront their own challenges.

To address this dynamic, it would be more beneficial for individuals to shift their focus from scrutinizing others to examining and improving their own lives.

This change could lead to greater self-awareness and empathy, fostering a more supportive and constructive environment.

By prioritizing personal growth over judgment, people can contribute to a more understanding and respectful society.

In time

In time, humanity will come to recognize the profound reality of Creation, understanding that they are the very life and spirit of it.

As stated in the teachings, their existence surpasses all conventional human thought and material states.

The physical condition of human beings is not their ultimate or final reality; rather, they possess a deeper essence within their physical lives.

This deeper essence is their true self, an immortal spirit that shines with an enduring light.

Unlike the physical body, which is temporary and subject to decay, this inner spirit remains unaffected by any external forces and is imperishable.

Although the planet itself will eventually face its end, the spirit within each person will persist indefinitely.

This immortal aspect of their being ensures that, even as the material world comes to an end, their true essence continues to exist.

Thus, humanity is more than just its physical form.

Their true nature is an eternal spirit, an aspect of themselves that remains alive beyond the lifespan of the physical world.

One's autonomy

For individuals to truly evolve, it is crucial to advance their consciousness continuously.

This ongoing development requires that thoughts be consistently nurtured & directed toward higher aspirations.

By dedicating themselves to this pursuit daily, people can foster significant personal growth.

It is equally important for people to affirm their control over their own lives.

This means recognizing that one is the master of shaping their personality, character, & moral values.

By embracing this self-awareness, people can actively engage in the constructive process of personal development.

Reaffirming one's autonomy is essential for personal growth & creativity.

Understanding that one has the power to influence their own path enables individuals to make intentional choices that align with their higher goals.

This awareness fosters a more purposeful & directed approach to life.

In essence, conscious self-direction is key to a fulfilling existence.

By acknowledging their role in shaping their own destiny, individuals can continuously strive for & achieve higher levels of personal & moral development.

This active engagement in self-improvement leads to a more meaningful & enriched life.

And so it is, as said prophet Billy in the teachings.

The Age of belief is over

The era of traditional thinking is coming to an end.

Previously, our approach to thinking was dominated by entrenched beliefs, which often impeded genuine cognitive processes.

Decisions were frequently based on assumptions & doubts rather than on rational analysis, leading to a distorted understanding of reality.

This flawed approach has fueled numerous conflicts, from international disputes to personal disagreements.

The New Age heralds a profound shift in how we perceive & engage with reality.

This transition promises to move beyond belief-driven thinking, enabling a more accurate & authentic comprehension of the world.

Significant contributions to this shift have come from the plejaren, particularly big thanks to Sfath, RIP, & Nokodemion, as embodied by Billy Meier.

Their efforts are instrumental in guiding humanity toward this new perspective.

Those who remain attached to outdated beliefs may struggle to adapt to the new reality.

According to Billy, the prophet of the New Age, this adaptation challenge is a natural part of the transition process.

As the old paradigms give way to new ways of thinking, those who resist change may find themselves at odds with the evolving understanding of the world.

The shift towards a new mode of thinking marks a crucial turning point for humanity.

By moving past limiting beliefs & embracing a more enlightened approach, we can address many of the conflicts that have historically plagued us.

This transition requires an openness to new ideas & a willingness to engage with a more accurate view of reality.

We are the ones we've been waiting for.

And we are here.

The awakening of the true ego

Human beings on Earth often perceive themselves solely through their material appearance, limiting their understanding of the physical realm.

Their true ego remains dormant, overshadowed by a material ego that governs their perceptions and actions.

This material ego is deeply invested in the tangible aspects of life and exerts considerable effort to cling to material possessions and experiences.

As a result, individuals remain under the influence of their material ego, which restricts their awareness of the superficial aspects of existence.

This focus on the material world prevents them from recognizing the deeper, more profound aspects of their true self and their connection to the larger fabric of life.

The awakening of the true ego marks a significant shift in consciousness.

When this deeper sense of self emerges, individuals begin to see beyond their material concerns and gain insight into their place within the broader mosaic of existence.

This newfound understanding fosters a more holistic perspective on life and one's role within it.

Truly, the awakening of the true ego enables a richer, more meaningful engagement with the world.

It allows individuals to transcend the limitations imposed by the material ego and to appreciate their interconnectedness with the greater whole, leading to a more profound sense of purpose and fulfillment.

Enemies

In life, it is essential to see that there are no true enemies; instead, focus on cultivating peace and harmony in every situation.

Understand that both positive and negative experiences come in succession, each serving as a lesson for your growth and evolution.

Acknowledge the equality of all individuals, recognizing that no one is above or below another, and maintain an unaffected stance toward external impressions.

Cultivate a mindset that values less materialism and more inner fulfillment.

When your heart is broken, approach the pain with gratitude for the lessons it offers and move forward without succumbing to sorrow.

Embrace full responsibility for your actions, as this is crucial for effecting positive change in your life.

Strive to adopt a logical and neutral approach in all matters, perceiving the love present in all living beings and in nature itself.

Celebrate the happiness of others with genuine joy and fearlessly confront the concept of mortality, understanding that your essence is eternal.

Reject belief in deities, recognizing that you are the master of your own life and actions.

Understand the interconnectedness of all beings and respect everyone's right to express themselves, regardless of whether you agree with their views.

Acknowledge that everyone has an equal right to share this Earth, and take responsibility for caring for the planet, which you will eventually leave behind.

Transcend national boundaries and view Earth as a collective home.

Find beauty in each person by looking beyond surface appearances and understanding the eternal nature of your soul and the cycle of reincarnation.

Comprehend the profound meaning of life and your role in the evolution of Universal Consciousness.

Empower yourself to make a positive impact and contribute to the betterment of the world.

Beyond control

It's important not to stress excessively over things beyond your control.

Embracing reality as it is, rather than forcing yourself into situations you cannot change, helps maintain inner peace.

When you resist accepting the unchangeable, you disrupt your own sense of harmony, leading to increasing frustration and anger.

This growing anger is detrimental to your mental well-being.

It creates a negative feedback loop, where your emotional state worsens as you struggle with things you cannot influence.

This constant internal conflict can be damaging to your psyche.

Furthermore, your inability to accept and adapt can also affect those around you.

The disharmony you experience internally can spill over into your interactions with others, creating a negative atmosphere.

This can strain relationships and impact your social environment.

Accepting reality and focusing on what you can change allows for a more balanced and harmonious life.

By letting go of the need to control the uncontrollable, you not only protect your own mental health but also contribute positively to the world around you.

800 years

On Earth, many people show a strong aversion to reading, preferring to attend weekly church services where others read the words of God to them.

These individuals, often referred to as "men of God," or whom I view as parasites, are handsomely rewarded for their services and live opulent lifestyles.

This phenomenon raises a fundamental question: why does this occur?

The root of this behavior lies in their perception of inadequacy and inferiority, which fosters a desire for a state of childlike dependence.

By calling themselves "children of God," they express this mindset, seeking reassurance from divine beings like God, angels, ancestors, and even deceased loved ones.

They rely on these entities for guidance and protection due to their perceived inability to manage life independently.

This reliance reflects a deep-seated belief in their own shortcomings and a need for external validation and support.

Consequently, they remain dependent on others to interpret spiritual and moral guidance rather than engaging directly with the texts themselves.

This dependency reinforces a cycle where self-reliance is diminished in favor of external authority.

As Billy Meier, the Prophet of the New Age, suggested, it will take humanity another 800 years to break free from this cycle of dependence.

Until then, this reality seems unlikely to change as the prevailing mindset persists.

Thus, the situation remains largely unchanged, reflecting a profound and enduring aspect of human behavior.

Satan

The concept of Satan relies entirely on belief for its existence.

If no one believed in Satan, there would be no reason for Satan to exist.

This implies that Satan is a product of human belief rather than an independent reality.

I am confident in my understanding of the Creation Energy Teachings presented by the Herald of this Universe, Billy Eduard Albert Meiert, commonly known as simply Billy, that Satan does not exist.

This conviction is also based on my personal thinking using logic & living in reality.

As a result, because I do not hold any belief in Satan, it has no presence in my life.

Thus, I render the idea of Satan irrelevant to my personal experiences & perspective.

Therefore, Satan does not factor into my life simply because I do not believe in it.

Without belief, Satan remains absent from my reality.

I take full responsibility for everything that happens in my life & so should you because such an entity does not exist.

According to the laws of evolution, your current personality represents the most advanced development of your creation energy.

This means that the traits and qualities you possess now are the result of a long process of growth and transformation.

Your present self embodies the culmination of all previous experiences and influences.

Given this understanding, it's crucial to recognize and embrace your evolved state.

Your personality at this moment reflects the peak of your growth journey, and this awareness should guide how you present yourself and interact with the world.

Embracing this evolved state means living in a way that is true to your most developed self.

It encourages you to act with authenticity and to fully utilize the strengths and insights that come with your current level of evolution.

Aligning your actions with this advanced state of being honors your growth journey and promotes continued personal development.

Strive to embody the highest expression of your creation energy, as this will lead to a more fulfilling and meaningful existence.

My evolution

At one point in my life, I saw myself exclusively as Haitian.

This identity shaped my experiences and how I connected with my heritage.

However, after moving to the United States, my self-perception evolved.

I began to see myself as a Black man, reflecting the new cultural and social dynamics I encountered in my new environment.

As time went on, this identification, too, began to fade.

I moved beyond seeing myself through racial or national lenses and started to view myself as a human being.

This shift allowed me to embrace a more universal perspective, free from the constraints of specific ethnic or racial categories.

Today, I consider myself a citizen of the world, with all of humanity as my tribe.

This expansive view has deepened my empathy and sense of connection with others.

When I see someone in pain, it affects me profoundly, as their suffering feels like my own.

Truthfully, my sense of identity has broadened to encompass a global perspective.

I now see all people as part of a larger human family, which profoundly shapes how I relate to and understand the world around me.

Applying the Creation Energy Teachings

Applying the Creation Energy Teachings is a simple process that anyone can integrate into their daily life.

The core principle is straightforward: practice living and letting live.

This means avoiding comparisons between your life and others and focusing on your own path.

Each individual is on a different journey, and it is best to concentrate on your own well-being while allowing others to do the same.

By not comparing yourself to others, you reduce unnecessary stress and anxiety.

It's important to remember that others' actions and decisions are their own business, not yours.

Keeping your attention on your own life and responsibilities helps maintain a healthier state of mind.

It is equally important to avoid aggression, as it disrupts your mental equilibrium and inner peace.

Aggressive behavior can interfere with your psychological balance, making it harder to achieve a sense of inner tranquility.

Maintaining a calm and balanced mindset is essential for personal well-being.

To live in peace and harmony, it is crucial to protect your inner peace.

By actively safeguarding this inner balance, you create a more serene and fulfilling life.

Prioritizing inner peace helps you handle life's challenges more effectively and contributes to a more harmonious existence.

Fame

I've never quite understood why someone would desire fame.

While I have no issue with how people choose to live, the idea of being constantly in the spotlight seems unbearable.

Life is about making mistakes and learning from them, but when every mistake is magnified under public scrutiny, it becomes nearly impossible to grow peacefully.

The pressure would drive anyone to insanity.

Fame, to me, is essentially giving up your life.

You lose the ability to enjoy life's simple pleasures because no matter where you go, everyone wants something from you.

There's no space to simply exist without being consumed by others' expectations or desires.

It's hard to imagine how anyone could truly live under those conditions.

In my view, famous people are often among the most miserable.

While they may appear successful on the surface, the weight of constant attention and lack of privacy takes a heavy toll.

Their lives are reduced to performances, stripped of genuine connections and the freedom to be themselves without judgment.

It's unfortunate that most people on Earth don't recognize this reality.

The allure of fame blinds them to its true cost, and they continue to chase it, unaware of the unhappiness it often brings.

Fame is seen as the ultimate goal when, in fact, it can lead to a life far removed from contentment.

Pain through guilt

Humans often appear to have a curious affinity for pain, frequently revisiting or contemplating thoughts that they know will cause them suffering.

This tendency can be traced back to deeply ingrained religious beliefs instilled from birth, beliefs that have been passed down through generations.

Such indoctrination creates a persistent cycle of guilt and self-inflicted suffering.

The religious teachings inherited from those who were similarly taught lead to a pervasive sense of guilt.

This sense of guilt can obscure their awareness of genuine happiness, as they are conditioned to focus on their own suffering.

Consequently, they may struggle to recognize or fully embrace moments of joy.

This ongoing cycle of guilt and pain makes it difficult for individuals to differentiate between suffering and happiness.

The constant emphasis on suffering and guilt often overshadows their ability to experience and appreciate positive emotions.

As a result, they may remain unaware of or unresponsive to their own happiness.

The interplay of inherited religious beliefs and a focus on guilt prevents many people from fully acknowledging or experiencing happiness.

The persistent emphasis on suffering, driven by deep-seated beliefs, can obscure their perception of joy and contentment.

True power

True power lies within each person's own Spirit-form or Creation Energy.

Recognizing and harnessing this inner strength is essential for overcoming obstacles and gaining wisdom.

The key to overcoming difficulties is understanding and utilizing one's own spiritual essence.

By trusting in this inner energy, people can gain the necessary knowledge and insight to handle life's challenges.

This approach emphasizes self-reliance rather than depending solely on external support like a god.

Such, truly, does not exist.

Prayers, if one chooses to pray, should be directed inward, focusing on one's own inner self rather than seeking help from external sources.

By connecting with their personal energy, individuals can access the guidance and support needed to navigate obstacles effectively.

This internal focus promotes personal empowerment and resilience.

The emphasis should be on harnessing the inner power and wisdom from the subconsciousness that each person possesses.

By relying on their own spiritual strength, people can address challenges and achieve growth more effectively than by depending on external means.

They came

Peace graced my presence, reminding me that calmness is possible even amidst life's storms.

It encouraged me to remain serene and composed, regardless of the chaos that may swirl around me.

Peace became a beacon of tranquility, guiding me through turbulent times with a steady hand.

Hope visited me as a guiding light, assuring me that better days are always ahead.

This presence instilled in me a sense of optimism, reminding me that hope is a constant source of strength and upliftment.

It helped me to trust in the future and the promise of brighter times.

Patience came to me, offering a gentle reminder that good things take time to come to fruition.

It taught me that growth and stability often unfold slowly and that the process is just as important as the outcome.

With patience, I learned to appreciate the gradual development of all things worthwhile.

Humility showed itself in a new light, teaching me that true humility is not about diminishing oneself but about focusing on serving others and lifting them up.

Through humility, I realized that greatness comes from contributing positively to the world and supporting those around me.

Accessible and actionable

The Creation Energy Teachings, delivered by the Universal Teacher and Herald of this Universe, offer a profound system for personal development.

These teachings provide a comprehensive understanding of the essential energies that govern our existence and empower individuals to master these forces.

By engaging with these principles, individuals can cultivate a deeper awareness of their own inherent capabilities.

The teachings are designed to be both accessible and actionable, allowing individuals to apply them in everyday life.

This process fosters significant personal growth and the ability to influence one's own path with greater intentionality and understanding.

Regardless of the current level of knowledge or experience, one can engage with these principles and work towards personal mastery.

The teachings support individuals in developing a profound connection with their inner selves and their spiritual journey.

In essence, the Creation Energy Teachings provide a pathway for individuals to achieve self-mastery and align with universal principles.

Embracing and practicing these teachings enables personal transformation, leading to a more harmonious and purposeful life.

This journey not only enhances individual well-being but also contributes to a greater sense of alignment with the broader cosmos.

The achievement

The achievement of one is the achievement of all.

When one of us "succeeds," it elevates the entire collective.

We are interconnected, and every individual's progress reflects the potential for growth and unity within the whole.

We must stop destroying one another.

By harming others, we are ultimately harming ourselves.

Every act of division weakens the fabric of our shared existence and leads to a cycle of pain that affects us all.

In truth, we are all one.

The distinctions between us are illusions that create unnecessary conflict and separation.

Beneath these differences, we share a common humanity bound together by the same essence.

Recognizing this oneness, it is clear that working together and supporting each other is vital.

To hurt another is to hurt ourselves, but to uplift one is to uplift everyone.

This shared unity is our greatest strength.

Sean Combs

Would you prefer your life as it is now or a life like Sean Combs?

It's natural to wonder about living someone else's life, especially one that seems filled with fame and fortune.

However, it's important to remember that life is not about comparison but about understanding and embracing the journey you are on.

Life is like a classroom where each person is enrolled in their own set of lessons.

While we may all be in the same school, no two students are learning the exact same material.

Your lessons are uniquely yours, just like a fingerprint, and they are tailored to your Creation Energy's growth and development.

Similarly, the lessons of others, no matter how glamorous or difficult their lives may seem, are meant for them alone.

Sean Combs may have wealth and fame, but those are simply the context for his own spiritual lessons, just as your experiences shape yours.

In the eyes of the spirit, social status or material wealth does not matter.

What is important is the progress made in learning the lessons life has to offer.

Everyone's path is equally valuable, and true fulfillment comes from accepting and growing through the experiences that are meant for you.

Misfortunes

Many Earth humans find satisfaction in witnessing the misfortunes of others.

This sense of enjoyment stems from a subconscious comparison between their own lives and those who are suffering.

Seeing others in unfortunate situations can create a false sense of superiority, leading people to believe their own circumstances are better by contrast.

This behavior is often fueled by insecurities and dissatisfaction with their own lives.

When people feel that their problems are insignificant compared to those of others, it can temporarily boost their self-esteem.

Instead of addressing their personal challenges, they may seek comfort in the idea that others have it worse.

Media and social platforms amplify this tendency by constantly exposing people to stories of hardship, tragedy, and failure.

These platforms thrive on human curiosity and the natural inclination to compare, making it easy for individuals to engage in this cycle of judgment and comparison.

In turn, this reinforces the belief that their own lives are more fortunate.

However, this mindset is harmful, both to individuals and society. Focusing on others' misfortunes prevents personal growth and perpetuates a lack of empathy.

A healthier approach would be to cultivate compassion and understanding, recognizing that everyone faces challenges and that true contentment comes from self-awareness and kindness, not from the suffering of others.

Political debates

Dear Earth people, to maintain your inner peace, it is essential to avoid becoming entangled in political debates.

Engaging in these discussions often leads to frustration and division, as each person holds a unique perspective that should be respected.

No amount of arguing will change someone's deeply held beliefs, and attempting to do so only disturbs your peace of mind.

The key to harmony lies in accepting differing points of view without feeling the need to challenge or change them.

When we respect others' opinions, we contribute to a more peaceful and cooperative world.

Political differences have existed for centuries, often leading to conflict, yet humanity continues to move forward regardless of these disagreements.

Rather than focusing on issues beyond your control, it is wise to distance yourself from the chaos of political strife.

Concentrating on the things you cannot change only drains your energy and distracts you from your personal well-being.

Life follows its own course, regardless of the heated arguments surrounding it.

Your true strength resides in your inner peace.

By protecting it, you cultivate a sense of calm and balance that allows you to navigate life more effectively.

In that peaceful state, your power and clarity emerge, enabling you to live harmoniously and with purpose.

After death

After death, the Creation Energy moves at the speed of light into "the beyond," a dimension located around the planet but separate from our physical realm.

In this space, the knowledge and wisdom gained from the most recent life are processed.

Once this transfer is complete, the material consciousness or personality that just lived is erased and transformed into pure energy.

This energy is then ready to be reprogrammed by the Overall Consciousness Block (OCB) for a new material consciousness and personality.

The OCB then prepares this energy for reincarnation, creating a new consciousness that is entirely distinct from the previous one.

When it reincarnates into a new human body, there is no connection to the former life.

The gender or skin color of this new body may be the same as before or entirely different, reflecting the unique circumstances of the new life.

Each incarnation is independent of the previous one.

As the new material consciousness takes form, it begins a fresh existence without any memories or attachments to its past incarnations.

The Spiritform or Creation Energy continues its evolutionary journey, acquiring new experiences and insights with each life.

The erasure of the previous personality ensures that every reincarnation offers a clean slate, providing opportunities for growth and development without influence from former identities.

It's crucial to remember that, regardless of physical differences like gender or skin color, all human beings belong to the same race.

These distinctions are merely part of our temporary physical forms and do not affect the underlying unity of our essence.

In the grand design of existence, we are all connected and share the same fundamental nature.

Countless times

We have all lived and died countless times, and yet we continue to exist.

Embracing this truth can fundamentally change the way we navigate life, allowing us to release feelings of hate, jealousy, and envy.

When we understand that we are part of an eternal cycle, we recognize that our lives and experiences are interconnected.

This realization leads us to see that everything in life truly belongs to all of us.

No single achievement or possession is isolated.

The success of one individual, in reality, contributes to everyone's well-being and progress.

We are not separate entities but part of a shared journey where each contribution adds to the collective experience.

In one lifetime, someone like Bill Gates may have founded Microsoft, but in the next, that could be your accomplishment.

The roles we play in life are ever-changing, and what one person achieves in this life, another may achieve in the next.

There is no need for envy or competition, as we are all participants in this infinite cycle of growth and creation.

By understanding this, we can live with a sense of unity and purpose, knowing that each person's success is, in truth, a success for all.

In recognizing the interconnectedness of our lives, we can let go of the illusion of individual ownership and embrace the shared reality that everything ultimately belongs to all of us.

In this life

In this life, I was born in Haiti because that's where my journey in my previous life came to an end.

And I'm a proud Haitian human being.

My rebirth in this land is tied to my Creation Energy's last stop, and wherever I meet my end in this lifetime, the next incarnation will likely begin in that place.

It's a continuous cycle where life and death are mere transitions across different regions of this shared planet.

Most of us have lived in different countries and experienced death in various lands.

We may not remember, but our Creation Energy has traversed borders countless times, inhabiting bodies in diverse cultures and societies.

If humanity understood this truth, the notion of belonging to just one country would fade, and the idea of fighting for national identity would seem senseless.

We are citizens of Earth, not just of nations.

The divisions we cling to, based on geography or nationality, would dissolve if we acknowledged our shared existence beyond borders.

Our experiences span continents, and our lives intertwine regardless of where we were born or where we die.

I see myself as a citizen of the Earth, not just of a particular nation.

Borders are just lines, but our connection to this planet is deeper than that.

We all share the same home, and our identities are not bound to a single country.

If we could truly understand this, we would stop seeing each other as enemies.

Every human being, whether they live near or far, is part of the same family.

We are all brothers and sisters, connected through life's cycles.

By embracing this truth, we could foster a sense of unity that transcends national boundaries, allowing us to live in peace with one another.

My advice

My advice is to begin detaching yourself from material wealth and embrace your true nature as a spiritual or Creation Energy being.

Material possessions can be a distraction from your inner self, and the more you cling to them, the further you drift from who you truly are.

Remember that your value doesn't come from what you own but from the depth of your spirit.

Let go of the need for external validation and focus on nurturing your inner world.

It's also essential to start being true to yourself and stop wearing the masks that hide your real emotions or intentions.

Pretending to be someone you're not only leads to dissatisfaction and unhappiness.

Authenticity is the key to personal freedom.

When you embrace who you are, you not only free yourself but also attract genuine relationships and experiences that resonate with your true self.

Another important step is to stop viewing others as enemies or threats.

Even if someone seems to be against you, remember that every person is a reflection of a shared human experience.

Instead of seeing conflict, view them as a part of yourself, deserving of understanding and compassion.

Rejoice in the presence of others—each encounter with another human being is a miracle, an opportunity for connection and growth.

Finally, learn to see everyone as part of your extended family.

Treat others as you would your mother, father, brother, or sister because, in essence, we are all interconnected.

Be patient with those who don't see things from your perspective, and give them the benefit of the doubt.

Life is unique for each person, with lessons and challenges tailored to their evolution.

Stop comparing your life to others and focus on your own journey.

Protect your inner peace at all costs, for it is the foundation of your growth.

Begin

Begin using the power of your consciousness by wishing for what you want, but don't merely believe it will happen—know it will.

When a person relies on belief alone, they only partially tap into their mental power.

Belief carries an element of doubt, which weakens the full potential of thought.

However, when a person begins to truly know who they are and recognize their inherent power, they access a much deeper strength.

This knowledge replaces doubt with certainty, allowing the individual to use their consciousness without limitations.

In this state, they unlock the full might of their thoughts.

When this realization occurs, the doors to the power of thought swing open.

The barriers that once held them back fall away, and they can shape their reality with confidence and clarity.

Their mind becomes a tool for creation, no longer constrained by the uncertainty that comes with belief.

Ultimately, the individual understands that they are the source of their own power.

They are not dependent on external forces but are the creator of their own life.

In this awareness, they recognize that they possess a divine ability, realizing that they are, in essence, their own god.

Same human race

We are all part of the same human race, as no individual on this planet possesses DNA exclusive to any one race.

The fact that we can interbreed across cultures and ethnicities is proof of our shared ancestry.

This interconnectedness highlights the common threads that unite us, regardless of how we choose to define ourselves.

Today, you might identify as a white man, but in another life, you could be born as a black man or woman.

Our potential to experience life from different racial perspectives emphasizes the insignificance of racial distinctions.

If humanity could embrace this truth, it could lead to a reduction in racism, as it reveals how arbitrary these divisions truly are.

Yet, despite this, we still face a long journey ahead.

Many people remain attached to outdated beliefs that hinder progress toward equality and unity.

These rigid ideas about race continue to fuel misunderstanding and conflict, keeping us from seeing the deeper truth of our shared human experience.

However, with persistence and patience, change is possible.

As more people come to understand the reality of our connectedness, the barriers that divide us will begin to weaken.

It may take time, but with determination, we can move closer to a world where differences in race are no longer a source of division.

The human body

The human body is a complex biological machine composed of organs, cells, and systems that work together to maintain physical life.

It operates through natural processes such as respiration, digestion, and movement, allowing us to function and interact with the world.

While the body is a material structure, its purpose goes beyond mere survival, serving as a vessel for higher consciousness.

What animates this biological machine is the Creation of Energy, a force that transcends the physical body.

This energy is the life force that breathes vitality into the body, making it more than just a collection of cells.

Without this energy, the body would be lifeless, incapable of thought, motion, or growth.

Creation Energy is the source that connects the material with the immaterial, bringing life into existence.

The material consciousness, or the mind, serves as the pilot of this biological machine.

It is responsible for decision-making, self-awareness, and guiding the body through its experiences.

The consciousness processes information from the body and the environment, shaping how we perceive and interact with the world.

As the pilot, it controls the machine, directing its actions and responses.

The ultimate meaning of life is to become one with this biological machine, mastering control over it.

This means aligning the mind with the body, learning to manage its impulses, and using it to achieve our highest potential.

When the material consciousness and the body work in harmony, we gain a deeper understanding of ourselves and our purpose, allowing us to fully experience and navigate life.

Focuss on the self

If everyone focused solely on their own lives, peace would prevail on this planet.

Many of the conflicts we face stem from individuals interfering in matters that do not concern them.

When we become preoccupied with others, we divert attention from the personal growth and responsibilities we need to address.

Our society tends to judge others without recognizing that true judgment lies within oneself.

Only the individual can fully understand their own life and be responsible for assessing their actions.

This failure to respect personal boundaries leads to unnecessary tensions and misunderstandings.

When we fixate on the lives of others, it often serves as a distraction from confronting our own flaws.

It's easier to point out someone else's mistakes than to reflect on where we may be lacking.

However, avoiding this self-reflection stifles personal evolution and fuels division.

In truth, your evolution is tied to your own life, not anyone else's.

By concentrating on your own growth and progress, you not only improve yourself but also contribute to a more peaceful and harmonious society.

Shackled mind

Religion has long shackled the human mind, limiting thought and progress.

It is time for it to be eradicated from the face of the Earth.

As many of us evolve beyond these ancient beliefs, we see that religion no longer aligns with the logic and reality we experience.

It has outlived its purpose and now only holds back our growth.

Welcome to the New Age.

The idea of God, as constructed by religion, is fading from the consciousness of humanity.

This process is inevitable, and no force can halt it.

As our collective understanding deepens, the grip of religious belief will naturally weaken and eventually disappear.

It is only a matter of time before humanity fully moves beyond the need for such concepts.

Indeed, there's no God above the human being.

For the sake of future generations, it is crucial that we keep religion away from children.

Allowing them to grow up free from its influence will enable them to think critically and embrace reason.

We must ensure that the next generation is not held back by the same outdated ideas that have restrained us for so long.

By doing so, we create the possibility of reincarnating into a world where religion holds less sway.

As society becomes less religious, the path toward a more logical, enlightened future will become clearer, allowing humanity to thrive without the restrictions of dogma.

My dedication

To me, the sharing of knowledge is essential, driving my commitment to freely impart everything I've learned.

This approach stems from a core understanding that knowledge should not be used as a means to elevate oneself above others.

Rather, I view knowledge as a communal resource meant to benefit and empower everyone equally.

I think that the pursuit of knowledge is not about personal advantage or superiority but about fostering collective growth and understanding.

By disseminating what I know, I strive to ensure a more equitable distribution of information, which can enhance lives and broaden perspectives.

This way of thinking shapes my interactions and collaborations, promoting a culture of openness and cooperation instead of competition or exclusivity.

I am convinced that the free exchange of knowledge helps to break down barriers, creating opportunities for learning and innovation that ultimately benefit society as a whole.

My dedication to sharing knowledge reflects a deep respect for the inherent worth and dignity of every individual.

By empowering others with the knowledge I possess, I hope to contribute to a world where everyone has the opportunity to thrive and share their unique talents and insights.

Wisdom of past lives

The teachings suggest that every human being carries within them the wisdom, knowledge, and experiences gained across countless lifetimes. This deep reservoir of understanding resides in the subconscious mind, largely dormant and untapped. Humanity has yet to master techniques of concentration that would allow individuals to access this hidden knowledge fully. If humans were to realize the power of their subconscious, they could unlock their full potential, gaining the benefits of everything they have accumulated through lifetimes. The subconscious holds not only information but also the abilities and wisdom needed to thrive and grow.

Within every person lies a profound longing to access this hidden wealth of knowledge and experience. People only need to recognize and accept its existence to benefit from it. Yet, accessing it requires an acknowledgment of a truth that goes beyond mere intellect: true understanding comes from both the material and the spiritual intellect working together. When this cooperation occurs, and the spirit is recognized as essential to self-awareness, individuals can reconnect with all they have gained in previous lives. This connection would enable them to approach life with deeper understanding and strength, drawing from a well of wisdom that spans multiple existences.

However, humanity often resists this knowledge, clinging to shallow perceptions and distractions. Overcoming these superficial tendencies is crucial; without spiritual insight, the material intellect is limited. For true self-awareness, people must go beyond physical reasoning and open themselves to the wisdom of their spirit. When individuals accept the reality of their spirit, they open the door to the knowledge accumulated across lifetimes. This reconnection provides the potential for personal growth and immense benefit, offering insights and powers that can transform their lives.

This wisdom and power, in fact, are humanity's Creational inheritance. These birthrights include knowledge, wisdom, power, freedom, and love, and they enable humans to serve as centers of influence in the world. Every individual has the potential to think deeply, to wield influence, and to inspire others. Recognizing one's own spirit and its abilities means understanding one's role in the larger framework of existence. With this awareness, humanity could contribute to a world marked by harmony and wisdom, where each person enriches the lives of those around them.

Personally, adopting this perspective means that I no longer rely on beliefs. Rather than "believing," I accept the truth within me. I trust that the wisdom of past lives exists within me, ready to be accessed when needed. This approach allows me to protect my inner peace, understanding that true power lies within. By maintaining this inner balance and acknowledging the strength of my spirit, I ground myself in a source of wisdom and power that transcends external influences.

Billy

Earth human beings have yet to reach their true potential as genuine human beings.

This is because, long ago, our DNA was altered in a way that made us naturally aggressive and inclined toward violence.

We were deliberately programmed to become warriors, creating a fundamental imbalance within us.

This genetic manipulation is humanity's original sin—a legacy of conflict and discord that continues to shape our behaviors and society.

The only way to undo this manipulation and free ourselves from this deep-seated aggression is through the Creation Energy Teachings.

These teachings offer a pathway to reconnect with the essence of Creation and to heal the imbalance within us.

By embracing this wisdom, Earth humans can gradually unravel the negative programming and realign with a higher, peaceful purpose.

It's a transformative process that requires dedication, self-exploration, and an understanding of Creation's universal laws.

In time, the world will come to recognize Billy and the significance of his work.

His teachings contain the keys to our evolution, guiding us beyond the limitations imposed upon us.

He has illuminated a path that allows humanity to reclaim its original state and move toward a harmonious existence.

Billy's legacy will inspire generations to come as they seek truth and strive for genuine human development.

For me, pointing others toward Billy and his teachings is not just a purpose—it's a profound life mission.

Nothing in my life feels more pressing or essential than this calling.

By introducing others to his knowledge, I hope to help them awaken to their true potential and begin their own journey toward freedom from the aggression programmed into us.

This mission is my contribution to humanity's transformation.

www.ingramcontent.com/pod-product-compliance
Lightning Source LLC
Chambersburg PA
CBHW051131120626
46547CB00012B/760